HALFWAY H

Ann & Scott –
Hope you enjoy these
stories of my "Journey."

Jackie K. Cooper
– 2005

HALFWAY HOME

THE JOURNEY CONTINUES

Jackie K. Cooper

By

Jackie K. Cooper

Mercer University Press
Macon, Georgia
25th Anniversary

ISBN 0-86554-972-9
MUP/H693

First Edition.

∞The paper used in this publication meets the minimum requirements
of American National Standard for Information
Sciences—Permanence of Paper for Printed Library Materials, ANSI
Z39.48-1992.

Library of Congress Cataloging-in-Publication Data
Cooper, Jackie K.
Halfway home : the journey continues / by Jackie K. Cooper.
p. cm.
ISBN 0-86554-972-9 (alk. paper)
1. Cooper, Jackie K. 2. Perry (Ga.)—Biography. I. Title.
CT275.C775142A3 2004
975.8'515—dc22
2004014588

For Walker Levi Cooper,

My grand grandson who holds the future.

ACKNOWLEDGMENTS

A book, though written alone, is a collaborative effort. At least in this case it is. I must thank Marc Jolley and the staff at Mercer University Press for their knowledge and their encouragement. Louann Lucas was tireless as a typist, while Ed Williams and Jackie White served as my pep squad. My "lunch bunch," which consists of Jackie, Cliff, Louise, Van, and Carol, are a part of this too.

It is great to have a family who believes in you, and I had that and more in the eyes of my wife Terry, my sons J. J. and Sean, my daughter-in-law Paula, and my grandchildren Genna and Walker.

And as always I have to thank my mother Virginia Kershaw Cooper who told me I was "special" and made me believe it.

CONTENTS

FOREWORD

By Terry Kay

author of *To Dance with the White Dog*
and *The Valley of Light*, among many other works of fiction.

Jackie Cooper has been having an affair and he's had the audacity to celebrate the consorting publicly.

The fellow is shameless about it.

The name of his mistress is Life, and if you want to read about her in all her glory—in work-day clothes and in finery—then stick with the pages following these words.

A warning, though: Jackie is a gentleman lover. You won't find the stuff of blackmail or water-cooler gossip. Truth is, some of it is as tame as pre-teen hand-holding, but also as delightful and as memorable.

Halfway Home (The Journey Continues) is an accounting, piece by piece, of Jackie's adventures during the years 1992-1995. The adventures have to do with people and experience—from Dolly Parton (who stunned him with her candor) to hypochondria (which he possesses)—and there's not a vignette in the entire book that fails to tickle an interest.

Such writing is not easy. It requires a light touch, control, and, above all, a love of the labor. Jackie only makes it look (or read) easy.

Let me address the love of the labor. I have known Jackie long enough to know he cares about words and he is a champion of those of us who try to fashion a living from making them. Any writer in Georgia is complimented by his approval, and his approval matters because those people who have been reading him for years trust him. Better still, they know him. They know his zeal, his passion, his integrity—all qualities that simmer in his stories like a rich broth in a good stew.

There is no reason for me, or anyone, to hand-pick and recommend from these offerings. To do so would suggest favoritism and that is not the purpose of reading such a book as *Halfway Home*. Let the reader decide. It's one of the things Jackie understands from his flirting years—Life dresses in many outfits.

So, read, enjoy. You've caught Jackie Cooper in his affair.

PROLOGUE

This book focuses on the years 1992–1995. This was one of the happiest times of my life—thus far. At this time I had just turned fifty, was happily married, had two great kids and a great cat, and was gainfully employed.

The world of this time was a simpler place. It was pre-9/11, which shall forever be the benchmark by which we mark the stages of our life. There was still an aura of safety around us, and to some degree an innocence.

I have gathered the stories I love from those years and in this book I tell them to you. They are presented in a conversational tone, just like it would be if you and I sat down to talk about this period of time. I would probably say to you, "Let me tell you a story," and off we would go.

So settle back and let the years wash over you. Get a cup of coffee, a comfortable place to read, and enter my world. I hope these pages take you back to places you might have forgotten and to people you might have lost contact with over the years.

Before we start on the stories, let me tell you how I came up with the title to my book. Back in the 1950s, whenever my family would travel, my mother would always want us to leave in time to be home before dark.

Sometimes that meant we got up and left on a journey just as the sun was rising. The miles would pass, and sometime during the trip my father would say, "We're halfway home and the sun's still shining."

My mother would always smile when he said these words for she knew he would get her home before it got dark. And he did.

Now so many years later those words still resonate in my soul. Just as all those "Walton" kids used to say goodnight in a comforting way, I cling to the beauty of my father's simple words, "Halfway home and the sun's still shining."

As I get older, I look on my life as a journey. It is a trip from birth to death and with a little luck the sun will shine on me all the way through the years. It has so far. I am a blessed man with a wife I love, two fine sons, and two precious grandchildren. The warmth from the sunshine of their smiles keeps me comfortable and content.

The years fly by like miles, and it seems I can now hear my father saying, "Halfway home and the sun's still shining." Am I halfway home? No one can answer that question. My journey could be over in the next instant or it could stretch for miles and miles, years and years. Still in my heart I think I am at the halfway point.

I don't look the same as I did a few miles back. My hair has thinned, and my waist has enlarged. I have wrinkles that are more than laugh lines. Still the sun is warm and my heart is happy. I am still enjoying the journey and I am full of anticipation for what lies ahead. I still look forward more than I look back. Some of my companions who were with me at the start have left my side, but I still have plenty of pleasant company as I travel.

I have hit some rough spots but that is to be expected. You can't always have the best of roads. Still it has been a journey well worth the taking and I can honestly say to myself, "I'm halfway home and the sun's still shining."

CHAPTER 1

REFLECTIONS FROM ROUTE 92

The Power of the Wind

There is something about the power of the wind that fascinates me. This is strange since I am such a coward when it comes to storms. Let the sky cloud up, I head inside, and I stay there until the storm has passed. But all the time I am inside I am wishing I was outside in the elements, feeling the wind on my face and its force all around me.

When I was about seven years old, I was caught outside in a windstorm. My brother and I had walked uptown by ourselves, and when we started home, a storm came up. It wasn't raining; there wasn't any lightning; it was just wind. And I loved it. The trees were bending over and the traffic lights were hanging sideways. Dust and debris were flying.

My brother stayed calm and that kept me calm as we made our way home. But when we got home my mother was almost hysterical. She just knew we had been blown off the face of the earth. Her alarm frightened me and I began to have pictures in my head of me and my brother being blown not only off our feet but off the planet. Maybe that was where my fear of storms began.

Recently, I have been reading about "storm chasers" who live in the Midwest. These daring souls chase tornadoes and watch as they touch down. They are not fascinated by the harm they do but rather by the power they possess. If I could be that brave, I would love to do something like that.

It would be amazing to witness the fury and power of a storm that forceful and that unpredictable. I would watch with awe as it became stronger and stronger, and I would be enthralled by the majesty of nature. Oh, if I could only be that irrational.

I am not alone in this wish. I have a friend who told me he would give anything if he could be out in the open when a tornado came. Now he isn't crazy. He wants to be guaranteed by God that he won't be hurt, and then he wants to feel all the storm's fury as it unleashes its power. He and I both agree that it would be an amazing feeling.

Jackie K. Cooper

3

I'm just not cut out to be a storm chaser. I am too practical. I know how deadly a storm can be and I respect my fears. I don't want to put my life at risk, for I intend to live to a ripe old age.

Still it would be a thrill. And there is something to be said for those people who are willing to take the high risks for the big thrills. They live to the fullest, but they sometimes die before their time. However, I bet when they go, they go with a smile on their faces and a mind that knows they lived, really lived, till that very last moment.

I love the power of wind. I am awed by windstorms. Maybe when I get to Heaven God will let me walk through one just for the fun of it.

Half Way Home

Another Side of Eden

When I was growing up I would listen to my father talk about his childhood and I wouldn't even recognize that life could be so idyllic and serene. He had lived at a time when his family got their water from a well, raised some of their food in the backyard garden, and the world was a poor but happy place to dwell. He didn't think of it as being a perfect childhood, but it sounded pretty good to me.

My childhood was not spent in a rural area. I grew up on Holland Street where children lived in abundance and life was protected and calm. There were about twenty kids in the Holland Street area and most of us got along. During the day we rode our bicycles or roller-skated, and in the evening we played baseball in the streets.

When I talk about it with my children they look at me like I lived on another planet. They just can't comprehend the freedom we had them. In the summertime, I would leave my house in the morning and wouldn't come back till lunchtime. Then I was out again and didn't come back till suppertime.

If my mother needed me she just hollered out the window. Sometimes her voice would not carry to where I was playing but people would hear it and pass along my name. It eventually reached me and when I answered, they would say, "Your mother's calling," and I knew to head home.

Most of the things we enjoyed doing didn't cost money. We played "roller bat" and shot marbles. Sometimes we even gave in to the girls and played hopscotch and jump rope. If it was raining we played Monopoly or Clue, or got out a deck of cards and played "Go Fish."

A lot of the time we just ran. We could be in the middle of some game and someone would say, "Race you!" and off we went. We ran up hills and down alleys. We ran through forests and over fields. We ran and we ran and we ran. Then we ran some more. I have never had so much energy.

Maybe everyone's childhood seems to have been perfect. I know mine certainly seems that way in retrospect. I don't remember any sorrow, any pain, any broken bones, any broken hearts. From birth till I was thirteen, my life was lead in another part of Eden.

It was only when the serpent named "cancer" came slithering into my mother's life that everything changed. My life is measured in terms of her illness, BC (Before Cancer) and AD (After Death). The years BC were perfect. The years AD were a struggle.

I hope that my children look back at their childhoods as a wonderful time. They didn't have the freedom we had. I was one of the most paranoid parents in the world—seeing danger in every stranger's face, and constantly in fear of harm to my kids. Still they did live through peaceful times.

My childhood was spent in another part of Eden. I wonder if any children will ever live there again.

We Are What We Speak

Years ago when I was a student in high school and college, I was blessed to have English teachers who raved on and on about the beauty of language. I didn't exactly comprehend at the time what they were talking about, but as the years passed I have learned what they were saying. Language is beautiful. It allows us to express ourselves and do so with impact and passion.

One thing that has made me aware of that is the exhilaration I receive from books. A well-written book can bring pleasures untold. And even a poorly plotted book can still provoke awe if it is written with skill. My favorite author, Pat Conroy, can do both.

If you loved the film *The Prince of Tides*, then you owe it to yourself to read the novel upon which it is based. And when you do read it, allow yourself the luxury of lingering over his phrases and descriptions. They are among the best ever committed to paper.

What worries me is that I don't think people read as much as they used to. Young people I talk with just don't have time to sit down and read a novel for pleasure. There is just too much else that has to be done. And if you don't read for pleasure you don't get the practice of good grammar and a good vocabulary.

I spent what seemed like hours the other day arguing with a friend about sentence structure. She was writing the phrase, "One of the best of the teachers are..." She said "teachers" made the verb have to be "are." I said "one" was the subject and "of the best of the teachers" were prepositional phrases and had to be ignored in deciding the subject. So it should be "one is..."

I finally convinced her, but it wasn't easy. She had in her mind that the noun next to the verb had to be the subject. That made sense to her and that is what she was going to use. Picky me just had to convince her otherwise. I even went so far as to diagram it for her with all those little lines sticking down for prepositional phrases and all the dividers between subject and verb.

Jackie K. Cooper

7

Do they still diagram like that in school? I hope so. It made it easy for me to remember and I think it did for everyone.

One last thought on this English lesson from Professor Cooper—what happened to not using profanity and expletives in mixed company, or not using them at all. I can't remember the last time I was in a business meeting and every word under the sun wasn't used. And a lot of the time women were the ones using the worst of them.

Now that sounds chauvinistic and I don't mean it to be, but when women decided they wanted the so-called rights of men I wish they had not taken the good and the bad. Some traits of women would have been better adopted by men and not vice versa.

I think maybe it is because we can hear any and all profanity in the movies we see. And a lot of the "bad" words can be heard on television. It is accepted today to talk in profane terms. And it is a sad commentary when we do.

I remember using profanity and shocking my parents with it. I thought it was a daring thing to do. After they recovered from the shock and after the punishment had been administered my mother told me that talking dirty was just being lazy. If I used my mind, she said, I could find ways to express myself that did not shock or offend others.

It's time for us all to clean up our acts—not be lazy in our talk or our actions. And just to make sure you know how to speak and write correctly, my advice is to read, read, read. You will learn a lot of what is correct by osmosis and that is the easiest way of all.

The Winning Team

It has taken me twenty-something years, but finally when someone asks me where I am from, I answer, "Perry Georgia." For the majority of my life when someone would ask me, I would respond, "Clinton, South Carolina." Well, I haven't actually lived in Clinton since 1967, and I have lived in Perry since 1974, so I guess Perry wins.

When I was growing up I always thought I would end up in some big place like New York or Los Angeles. Those were cities that were alive and offered art and culture and adventure. That was then and this is now. The biggest place I want to be around is Atlanta. When I make a trip to LA or NY, it is a quick one.

There are a zillion advantages to living in a small place and a trillion to living in Perry. The main one is the sense of belonging that a small community gives to you. Never do I get that community sense more than at a sports activity for one of the high school events.

My youngest son, Sean, is into sports and plays them all. My wife and I survived the football season this year, but just barely. We had dreams of injuries and other cataclysmic events. Thank God they didn't happen. Now with that behind us we had a break and have moved on to baseball. Sean has only played four games so far but they have been exciting, exhilarating, and *freezing*! Do you know how cold it gets out on a baseball field? I thought I was going to die.

At the last game I wore a shirt, a sweatshirt, and a hat. Plus I had another sweatshirt around my waist. That was the spare one I was going to put on if it got any colder. My son and my wife have threatened me with my life if I ever go to a game looking like that again. I didn't see anything wrong with it, but Terry said the shirts looked ridiculous, and Sean said the hat had to go.

It wasn't really a hat, just a cap. People wear them all the time and no one fusses at them. But Sean and Terry said the cap sat on my head at a strange angle and made me look goofy. That was the exact term—goofy!

Jackie K. Cooper

Anyway, I stayed warm and when the game started I had a great time. I know that involvement in sports builds camaraderie among the players, but it does a heck of a lot for the parents too. If you have a child playing on a team and you do not go and watch and support him or her, you are depriving yourself of some great joy.

Once you get a bunch of adults on the sidelines cheering for their team, you have something akin to a family unit. You worry if some one gets physically hurt, you worry if someone is not playing their best, and you worry if someone's feelings are going to get hurt by a bad call. You worry as a group, and then you win or lose as a group.

At one of the first games my son got a hit that brought in the winning run. It was wonderful. I was on "Cloud Nine." I wouldn't have missed it for anything. The sad thing is that I could so easily have missed it. There were things at work I thought I couldn't put off. There were other things I thought I would rather be doing than sitting out in the cold and watching a high school baseball game. There were lots and lots of reasons not to go. And only one reason to go—and that was Sean.

When he made that hit and when all of us parents jumped around and hollered at the win, it was heaven come to earth. And it wasn't just the winning; it was the thrill of the moment. The happiness you get for your child, or you get for someone else's child who has had a moment of glory.

I was happy. Terry was happy. Sean was happy. Everybody on our side was happy. That's the way we are in the town where we live. We share life. And when it is good, there is nothing that can compare with the joy of many hearts in unison feeling good about a common achievement.

Good Golly, Miss Dolly

I have always loved the movies, and I have always looked up to those people who were my heroes on the silver screen. From the Lone Ranger to John Wayne, I thought the stars who played the roles were as heroic as the roles they played. As I grew older I found that in many, many cases that is not true.

But every once in a while you get a chance to meet someone who is everything you had hoped they would be and more. That happened when I was invited to Atlanta to see Dolly Parton's new movie and to have an interview with the lady herself.

The movie's title is *Straight Talk* and it is the best Dolly Parton movie ever. Now I don't mean it is better than *Steel Magnolias*, but it is a better role for Dolly. In this one she is funny, pretty, and just all round great.

Still the thrill of the day was getting to meet this superstar in person. I have been a Dolly fan for years and years and years. I go all the way back to when she was Porter Wagoner's sidekick. At that time I didn't even care anything about country music. I just knew she was a fantastic looking woman with a unique personality and a certain charisma all the truly big stars have.

She also appeared to be completely unaffected by all the hoopla and hype about her appearance and her personality. If ever a personality appeared to be truly down to earth it was Dolly. Now having met and talked with her, I can happily tell you that with Dolly what you see is what you get.

And what do you see when you see Dolly in person. Well today's Dolly is at a healthy looking weight. No more the emaciated star who looked like a poster child for anorexia. Her health problems are a thing of the past and she is content with how she looks and feels.

On this day she is dressed in jeans and a jeweled jacket. When questioned about the jacket she replied that her sister runs a boutique in Nashville and she gets a lot of her clothes there. Not only does she like the clothes her sister carries, but she also likes the idea of being

Jackie K. Cooper

able to help her out with an endorsement of sorts. So from this you gather that family is still at the top of Dolly's list of priorities.

Family also includes her husband Carl, the mystery man that many—myself included—have thought doesn't even exist. But Dolly insists he does. They have been married for 20-something years now and from her way of talking about him, it is a marriage that is for keeps.

Her commitment to marriage like her religion seems to be deeper than it appears to be on the surface. She began to talk about religion when I asked her about the song "He's Alive" that appears on her last album. It is a deeply felt religious song that will give you chills when you hear it.

I had heard that the choir from the Judds' church appears as backup for her on that song and I asked her about that. She replied that the choir is from a prominent church in Nashville where a lot of performers go each Sunday. She said it was her sister's church but not hers. I liked the way that sounded. I mean that is the way people I know talk. They say such and such church is their neighbor's church, or their church, or somebody else's church. It is a statement of possession.

On that day in Atlanta Dolly looked like a million dollars and acted like 29 cents. That doesn't mean she acted cheaply in any way. What I mean is that she was down to earth.

I know she probably wouldn't remember me if we ever had the chance to meet again, but on that day she acted as if we were great friends. On my part we are. In this day and time when so many people we admire turn out to be so much less than what we expect, it was wonderful to meet someone who was everything I wanted and more.

Take it from me, Dolly is a delight—full of homespun humor and straight talking sass. She's a superstar who has her little tiny feet planted firmly on solid ground. The first thing she said to me was that I could ask her anything and she would answer it. I hesitated, trying to figure out my first best question.

She looked me straight in the eye and said, "Yes, they are real. Now let's move on." And we did.

Half Way Home

Mary Kate

They say in life there are only two sure things—death and taxes. In this month of April I have had to face both. The taxes I can understand. The death of a person I love, I can't.

Mary Kate is a person I have loved most of my life. She is the mother of my best friends from high school—Lyllis and Hollis. When I lost my mother to cancer I sought a substitute family from which to draw love and strength. Mary Kate took me into hers and made me feel wanted.

Mary Kate was probably one of the first adults I called by their first name. She wasn't even Miss Mary Kate, which is the way nice Southern boys sometimes addressed adult ladies. She was just always Mary Kate, and I said it with all the respect possible in the world.

There were many times when I would go to Hollis's house and neither he nor Lyllis would be home. Mary Kate and I would sit and talk and be wonderfully happy. It was Mary Kate who taught me to play bridge. She couldn't persuade Hollis or Lyllis to play, but I was a willing pupil.

Her teaching me to play had an ulterior motive. Once I had learned, I was dragged in as a player any time her bridge club met and they needed a fourth to fill a table. I was young and had a lot of free time on my hands, so I was a willing party.

The wonderful thing about Mary Kate was that she was an adult, but she was always young at heart. She didn't try to pretend that she was a teenager like we were. She just had a youthful way about her that made her acceptable to me and Hollis and Lyllis's other friends.

Mary Kate's husband was a traveling salesman and didn't get home that often. So I never knew him like I knew her. I do know that his absences were hard on her and that she had a lonely life of sorts.

After I went off to college Mary Kate and her husband moved to Kentucky. They came back to South Carolina on the day Hollis and I graduated from college. That was the last time I saw her. In all the years that passed I kept thinking one day I would see her again, but I didn't. But I did keep her in my mind and heart. My parents called me a few weeks ago to tell me Mary Kate had died. The funeral was going to be in South Carolina the next day. My schedule was such that I couldn't go. All I could do was send some flowers and put "Love, Jackie" on the card.

It bothered me that a person so vital to me at a crucial period of my life was gone. I wondered if she would be remembered by those who felt the influence of her life. And I regretted that my own family had not had the pleasure of her company.

A few nights later at the supper table I began to tell stories about Mary Kate and how funny she was, and how much fun she was. My youngest son, Sean, always likes for me to talk about the old days, so he eats up these "old tales" of mine.

As I talked about Mary Kate I realized that as long as people do remember her, she will always live. Now that I have passed some of the stories about her on to my family she will live in their minds too.

In many instances a person only lives a brief time on this earth, while in the case of Mary Kate it was seventy-something years. It isn't the length of the life but the impact for good it has on one person or a hundred. Mary Kate left me with a legacy of love. I will miss her, but I still have her memories in my heart and in my mind. As long as I live, those memories will never die.

Half Way Home

A Prayer For Beasts and Children

Whenever I hear the phrase "bless the beasts and the children," I smile. It has always been a particular favorite of mine. I have always considered it as half thought and half prayer, for it recognizes that these two categories cannot help themselves and prays for God's watchfulness over them.

This past weekend it especially came home to me. It was junior/senior dance weekend at my son's school and that means a dance and some parties afterwards. Now I want my son to enjoy all the events of life, but I want to be able to keep his safety absolutely under my control. Still, unless I wanted to hang like an albatross around his neck, all I could do was sit at home and worry. My wife and I did manage to go out to the high school and sit in the bleachers and watch a few moments of the dance. And before that, my wife did manage to corner him and his friends for a few pictures. We also did have him call home before he went to the after-dance breakfast, and then when he left the after-dance breakfast, and when he left to go to a second party at a friend's house, and when he left to come home from that party.

It wasn't that I didn't trust him. I do completely. It is just those other idiots in the world who are out there driving drunk or acting crazy in some other ways. I want to protect my children from them.

But you can't be with your children all the time. You have to develop trust in the way they conduct their lives and hope all the lessons you have tried to teach them have taken. Finally, you have to believe in the power of prayer and then practice it over and over and over.

Even with my faith intact, I don't think I really slept any that Friday night. It wasn't until I got Sean home and locked the door behind him that I really felt safe again. Then I slept.

Later that afternoon while I was sleeping, someone came over to visit with my wife. I didn't even know they had come. She told me about it while we were eating supper. And while we were eating supper I asked her where Fluff, our "beast" was.

She wasn't in all her regular hiding places. And she didn't come running even when we shook her box of food. This is always the surefire way of getting her attention. She responds to food even when she won't respond to our voices. But this time there was no answer from her.

Finally I opened the back door and hollered. Here she came like a streak across the backyard, and up into my arms she jumped. Honestly, her eyes were the biggest I have ever seen on a cat. They were the eyes of a terrorized being.

Obviously she had slipped out the door when Terry had company. She likes to do this, but she always relies on the fact we will see her and bring her back in to the house.

This time Terry didn't see her go out and the door was shut behind her.

Thank goodness nothing happened to her. She is in the house now, asleep at my feet as I write this. I have talked with my older son at college and he is doing okay. Sean is asleep in his room. I am a happy man. God has blessed my "beast" and my children, and kept them safe for me.

Graduation Day

Each year at graduation time I think of a song that symbolizes the climate of the world they are entering. This year's theme song for the graduating class could certainly be "Is There Life Out There?" It seems just as these high school seniors are getting ready to walk down the aisle and receive their diplomas, the world is going crazy. Small wonder many of them would like to just say thanks but no thanks and stay in high school another year.

From the riots in Los Angeles to the birth of Murphy Brown's baby, this is a time of questioning and doubting. A lot of the old-time traditions are falling by the wayside, and confusion about who we are and what we are run rampant. It is not the best time to be facing the world.

Still I remember back over all the span of years to my high school graduation. I don't remember being real sure about what I was getting into either. I had been going to school with this group of people since kindergarten and during the four years of high school we became really close. I wasn't sure I wanted to go off to college and meet a new set of good friends. The old ones suited me just fine, thank you very much.

As I stood in the wings waiting to march on to the graduation stage I was young, happy, and in love. I think most seniors are young, happy, and in love. I remember that right after graduation, Elaine, my longtime girlfriend, told me she would love me forever (she didn't). I also remember one of my good friends, Jimmy Young, told me we would be friends forever (we weren't). So accept it, seniors, you are going to hear some lies in these few days of celebration.

Even with those two failed relationships I still look back and find high school gave me my greatest sense of worth as well as the special time that I needed to prepare me for the world. Out of that time I gained two of my best friends, Hollis and Chuck, and they are still two of my best friends today. Anybody who went to high school with me holds a special place in my memory.

Jackie K. Cooper

That is not true of college. I liked college, but it was more of a serious time. I had to study in college. I hadn't had to study that much in high school. Plus high school was a place where you could be just plain silly and it didn't matter. In college you could act a little crazy, but you couldn't be just silly.

It's odd how the mind works. I don't remember many specifics from college, but I could quote you entire conversations from high school. I can name every couple from our senior class and could just about tell you when they started dating and who went with whom before that time.

High school years for me were the 1950s. Those were the Eisenhower years and a time of tranquility for the entire country. College was the 1960s and that brought Vietnam and other national tragedies. It was the real world, the cold world, and in many cases the cruel world.

But for all the fears high school seniors might have today, the future really is theirs. They can make it, mold it, advance it and enhance it in any and all ways they deem necessary. Once again we are offering to tomorrow the best and the brightest we have to share.

Graduation day is a time for change. The departing seniors have left their footsteps in the sands of time, and they are embarking on the first day of the rest of their lives. There is life out there, life to be lived to the fullest and loved to the hilt. Their parents, family, and friends offer them Godspeed and add a silent thanks for the memories.

Seeing the Positive In the Negative

Sometimes I look in the mirror and see my father's face. Or rather I see the face he had when he was a middle-aged man. That is the image I have most of my father. When he was in his forties, and still robust and athletic.

Those are the best memories of my father, for when he was that age my mother was still alive, and we were still a united family. My brother and I were both living at home and neither death nor college had separated any of us.

My father drove a bread truck back then and he worked from sunup to sundown, six days a week. How he did it I'll never know. But he did. And he didn't complain about it. It was just his job and he worked his job in order to provide for his family.

One of the most prominent features of those recollections was of the way my father smelled after he came in from a hard day's work. It was a sweet smell of sorts. Not offensive, just a sweet, sweaty smell that was uniquely his.

I loved that smell, and when I would run up to hug him that was the first sense that came to me—how good he smelled.

Later when I was out of school and getting ready to be married I noticed that my father was no longer as young as he used to be. His hair was a little whiter, and he didn't move as fast. But he still was healthy and full of life. Even when he had prostate cancer his optimism did not leave him.

I think that is when he surprised me the most, for I thought I knew him pretty good. Therefore, I thought the knowledge that he had cancer would sink him. But it didn't. He faced it with courage, Christian strength, and the conviction he was going to get well. And he did. I had sold short his strength of character and I was wrong.

After my father retired from his job as a bread salesman he went to work for my cousin who has a car dealership in South Carolina. My father would deliver cars, run errands to the bank and post office, and do other things that just needed to be done. He has done that for sixteen years.

But this week my cousin called me and said he was going to have to stop using my father at his place. My cousin said my father's driving had gotten too dangerous and that he couldn't be responsible if he hit someone or caused an accident.

I understood what my cousin was saying, but I dreaded the thought of how my father would react. But once again he fooled me. He called me after he and my cousin had had their talk, and he said he was okay. He added that he knew that he had to slow down some, but quickly added that he would still be going up to the car place to see everyone. As my cousin had said, he still had "full showroom privileges."

I have watched my father's life go through many stages and transitions. Each time he faces an obstacle that I think will do him in, he steps back and finds something to encourage him. Plus, he still finds something to look forward to in each new day.

He may not be working for my cousin anymore, and he regrets that. But now he says he and my stepmother will do more things together and won't be tied down. There is a plus to the minus. There always is, in his eyes.

All of us are going to get older—if we live. And as we get older there are going to be some tough times. I just hope the ability to find the positive in the negative has been passed on to me through my father's genes. He may be older and more frail now, but he still has a toughness of spirit. That is what I hope I have inherited.

Bobbie Eakes

It was several years ago I first saw and heard a young girl stand up on a stage and sing her heart out about tomorrow and how great it was going to be. Yes, that was my introduction to the magic that was and is Bobbie Eakes.

I had just started writing for various newspapers in the area and one of the assignments I drew was to review the Warner Robins High School "Follies." This musical extravaganza, which was created by teacher Ronnie Barnes, was known far and wide as a showcase for phenomenal young talent.

Being a Perry resident, I was not really aware of who were the "stars" at Warner Robins High School during this time. Once I got to the show however I found out but quick. Ronnie had built most of the show around the Broadway play "Annie," and Bobbie Eakes was cast in the title role.

When she first entered onstage she was pretty and composed. I was impressed. When she opened her mouth and sang she was amazing. I was stunned. I had never, ever known local talent could be so good. But she was. And as she sang the song about "Tomorrow," which is Annie's anthem, I knew that her career could take her as far and as high as she wanted to go.

A few days after the "Follies" had ended my wife and I were in McDonald's and there was Bobbie. She was working part-time to make some extra money. The fact she had been a "star" a few days before didn't mean that she was above cleaning some tables to earn some extra money.

Through the years I have found this duality perfectly epitomizes Bobbie. She has the talent to do wonderful things and she has the drive to work hard and make these things happen. That drive has taken her through school and pageants and all the way to Hollywood.

Since she has been living in California, I haven't seen her as often as I would like. It is through her parents, her sisters, and the movie magazines on the shelves at the local supermarket, I have learned about her career and how it is progressing.

Plus, I have seen her on commercials and some nighttime shows. Because of my work schedule I don't get to watch her regularly on "The Bold and the Beautiful" where she stars as Macy.

In all the years I have know the Eakes family, I have marveled at how normal they are.

In a family that has known an enormous amount of adulation and praise, each and every member acts as down to earth as you or me.

They are proud of their accomplishments, but they are not boastful about them; and the parents, who must be overflowing with pride, still present the image of a typical mom and dad, who think their kids are pretty great.

Being the romantic I am, I always hoped that Bobbie could balance a career and a family. I knew it would take a very special man to become part of her life and I prayed God would send him to her as soon as possible.

Well, my prayers have been answered, and even though I don't know David Steen, I hear he is every bit as special in his way as Bobbie is in hers.

A few weeks ago, I received a wedding invitation in the mail. It invited me to the wedding of Bobbie Eakes and David Steen on 4 July 1992.

When it took place, Terry and I were there and it was everything a wedding could and should be.

Since Bobbie is one of our most prominent celebrities, the three questions I have been asked most about the wedding are: (1) Did Bobbie make a beautiful bride? (2) Did any of the cast of "The Bold and Beautiful" come? And (3) What about David Steen?

Here is the Jackie Cooper report on those three issues. Believe me when I say that Bobbie Eakes made a supercalifragilisticespialidotiously beautiful bride. She looked like something straight off the cover of *Brides* magazine. When the back doors of the church opened and she started down the aisle you heard one collective "ooooh" go up from the crowd. She was stunning!

Now as to "The Bold and the Beautiful" contingent. The cast was well represented with a group from Hollywood. I never did get their "real" names so you will have to accept that "Thorne," "Sally," "Clarke," "Sol," and "Felicia" were all there. From what I know of the soap these are the people who are associated most with the character of "Macy" that Bobbie plays on the show.

My wife and I were fortunate to be invited to the rehearsal dinner and so got to see them up close and personal. The strongest impression I got from all these people is what good sports they are. When they arrived at the NCO Club at Robins AFB, it was as though the European Paparazzi had descended on them. I never saw so many people with cameras in one place. And all of them wanted to take pictures of the stars, have pictures taken with the stars, or just talk to the stars. All five of the Hollywood group were gracious to each and every person who approached them.

Now for the final question, what about David Steen? The answer is that he truly does seem to be the perfect match for Bobbie. His father had asked us to come to the rehearsal dinner so that we could learn something about David and we certainly did. We learned it from the toasts and comments offered up by his friends and relatives.

Each of the six men who were David's groomsmen made comments during the night at the rehearsal party. Each in their way told of how special he is as a friend and how talented he is as an artist. They believe in him as a man and as a playwright, and feel he and Bobbie will complement each other's life.

Then there was Leroy Steen, David's dad. This man missed his calling—he should have left Memphis and the business world and moved to Hollywood and been a stand-up comic. He was hilarious. He had everyone in the room in tears—tears of joy and laughter—as he told one funny story after another.

But funny or not, the overall message was that the merger of the Eakes/Steen clans is going to be a wonderful one. These two traditional American families have each raised wonderful children and the marriage of Bobbie and David is the fruit of their labors.

So from my perspective it is wonderful to toast parents who take on the stages of life with acceptance and enthusiasm; parents who raise children who succeed in their professional and personal lives; and young people who wait for the destined right person to come into their lives. The Fourth of July 1992 was a time for Happy Birthday, America; and God bless you, David and Bobbie. The best is yet to come.

An Atlanta Adventure

You never know when your feet hit the floor in the morning what events are going to come your way during the hours of the day. If we knew, we just might get back in bed and pull the covers over our heads.

For example, last Tuesday started out like any ordinary day, but it didn't end up so ordinary. It ended up with my life being risked and my property being damaged. There's certainly nothing ho-hum about that.

This life-threatening event happened when I drove to Atlanta to preview a movie and interview a celebrity. I had been invited to come to the Ritz-Carlton in Buckhead, go out to see the movie *Rapid Fire*, and then interview the star of the film, Brandon Lee.

It was going to be a great day and a half and I was excited about it all.

On Tuesday afternoon I even managed to make it through downtown Atlanta without too much trouble.

All the heavy traffic appeared to be heading south while I was heading north., but when I got within a mile of the Buford Highway exit off the interstate, traffic came to a complete stop.

Still I wasn't upset. I had thirty minutes before I was due at the hotel for registration, so I could afford a few minutes stuck in traffic. I turned on the radio and smiled as Mary Chapin Carpenter began to sing "I Feel Lucky." I had to agree with her that I felt lucky too.

As Mary Chapin and I sang beautiful harmony I suddenly felt as if I was in one of those bumper cars at the county fair. I was smacked in the rear by a strong impact and pushed towards the car in front of me. My foot instantly went to the brake and the impact in front was much, much less than the impact in back.

When everything came to a stop I got out of my car and looked behind me to see what had happened. A young man was headed my way saying, "I'm sorry! I'm sorry! It was my fault!"

Jackie K. Cooper

I had to feel sorry for him because it was obvious he had not been watching and had just plowed into me. The couple in the car I had been pushed into got out and joined the gathering on the interstate. Meanwhile other cars whirled and sped around us, trying to keep moving while we caused a delay.

In a short time a policeman arrived and helped us get all three cars off the interstate and on to the side of the road. My car was obviously the most injured of the three. It had a lot of damage in the back and the left bumper was scraping against the left rear tire.

I was pleased to hear that the young man was still giving his litany of obligation.

While the policeman was sending in information on all three cars, the young man kept repeating how sorry he was and that he had had his mind on his sick girlfriend.

I memorized all these statements in case we ended up in court.

Finally, the policeman came back and gave me and the couple a notice to appear in court as witnesses to the accident. He then handed "Mr. sick girlfriend's boyfriend" a ticket for reckless driving. He said if the insurance company paid off ok, the witnesses would not have to appear in court. The reckless driver would.

This being over, the other two parties got in their cars and left. The policeman and I stayed to wait the arrival of a tow truck. It took forever, or at least a half-hour, whichever is longer.

Finally the tow truck came, hooked up my car, gave me the address where it would be located, and drove away leaving me and the policeman on the side of the interstate. I must have looked like some dejected mess for the policeman kindly asked, "Can I take you anywhere?"

I had to get to the Ritz Carlton in Buckhead, so I asked the policeman if he could take me there. He hesitated for a second and then said, "I don't know anything about that part of Atlanta. I drive over here every day from Heflin, Alabama, and I just know the part of Atlanta that is in my patrol area. That area ends at the Buford Highway."

I assured him that I could direct him to the Ritz Carlton and then could send him back to the interstate so he wouldn't be lost. He

Half Way Home

agreed, so I picked up my bags and headed towards the front seat of his police car.

"Uh, uh," he said when I opened the front seat door. "It's against the law for you to ride in the front seat. You'll have to get in the back."

So I got in the back. The infamous backseat where heinous criminals have been placed. The place where you can't open the doors from the inside and where a wire screen separates you from the front seat.

I instantly had an attack of claustrophobia. I also instantly wondered what would happen if this policeman had a wreck and I was trapped in this back seat. What if the car caught on fire and I was inside. What then! As you can tell, I have a vivid imagination.

Anyway I would rather be in the backseat of a police car than standing on the side of the road in Atlanta, so I considered myself lucky and concentrated on the ride. The thought did go through my mind, however, that I hoped no one I knew happened to see me in the backseat being transported through the city.

As we got closer to the Ritz Carlton, it dawned on me that maybe, just maybe, the people at the sedate establishment would prefer their guest not arrive in police cars. I could just imagine the doorman gulping when the police car cruised up to unload me. At this point I decided it would be a wise thing to have the policeman let me out in the parking lot of the Lenox Mall. Then I could walk across the street to the Ritz Carlton and they and I would be spared further embarrassment.

So this is what I did. I thanked the policeman from Heflin for the ride. He got out and let me out (a sigh of relief there!) and I hauled my bags over to the Ritz.

During all the time of the accident and aftermath I had thought I was wonderfully calm about the whole thing. I had not fallen apart. I had not sat down on the roadside in a crumpled heap. I had been cool, helpful, and not the least bit panicky. Therefore, it came as a complete shock to me that I could hardly sign my name when I went to the registration desk at the hotel.

I am sure I looked like a sweaty mess and when the chipper young man asked me how I was doing, I came back with a quick "I've had a wreck!" I then proceeded to tell the group of people assembled there all about my experience. Their eyes glazed over as I ranted and raved. And finally when I was supposed to sign in my hand wouldn't work. It was shaking so hard I could barely hold the pen. I was having a delayed anxiety reaction.

I continued to shake as I made my way to my room. I am sure I looked like an Elvis impersonator in full performance. Thankfully the rest of my stay in Atlanta went off without incident.

When I was ready to leave the Ritz Carlton, I took my bags downstairs and asked the doorman to get me a cab. I told him I needed to go to Milton Avenue, which is where my car had been towed. He went over and talked with one of the cab drivers and came back and told me he had taken care of everything.

The cab driver drove to where I was and I got in. I asked him if he knew where Milton Avenue was, and he nodded his head in a positive manner and we took off. I guess he indicated in a positive manner. With all the dreadlocks going up and down I could only assume it was meant to be "yes." And in a few minutes he told me, "Don't worry, Mon. I know de Lanta."

So off we went through the streets of Atlanta. At least we did get to the stadium area in a very short time, but once we got there it was obvious my Mon did not have any idea where Milton Avenue was.

Finally a light bulb went off in his head and he hollered, "Just two more streets, Mon. I know de Lanta." Two more streets and we landed on Martin Avenue. "Not Martin," I reminded him, "Milton!"

"Oh yes!" he replied. "You want to go to Milton. Don't worry Mon. I will get you there." And after three stops to get directions we did get to the place where my badly damaged car was sitting.

Mon decided he would stay with me until I found out about my car. And, in truth, it gave me comfort to have him there. He might not know all there is to getting around "de Lanta," but he was friendly and I was really feeling alone. And at this wrecking place, they were not in a very good mood.

Half Way Home

I asked the lady in charge if someone could try to pry the bumper off my back wheel, so I could drive the car home to Perry. She looked at me as if I had asked her to carry my car home on her back. "Ain't nobody messing with that car out there," she said. "If I have somebody touch that car the insurance company will be down on my neck."

By this time desperation was setting in on me big time. I was stuck in Atlanta without a car and the only friendly face was Mon's bright one, which kept a continual smile. Like Scarlett O'Hara yearning to get back to Tara, I thought if I could only get home to Perry everything would be all right again.

Finally, a man at the wrecker place told me he could have the car towed to Boomershine Motors and I could get a rental car there. He said Boomershine was located on Spring Street. I asked Mon if he knew where it was and he replied—You guessed It—"Yes, Mon. I know the Boomershine. It is here in de Lanta."

So off we went once more. Me and Mon and his trusty cab. Two more stops for directions and about twenty-five minutes later we crested a hill and below us was the Boomershine sign. "See, Mon," he shouted, "I told you I know de Lanta."

At Boomershine I got a rental car and I got assurances that my car would be repaired. In record time I was ready to head back to Perry. And only then did Mon leave me. He had stayed with me the whole time I was signing the rental car papers and talking with the Boomershine people.

Ok, so Mon wasn't the best cab driver the city of Atlanta has to offer. That isn't the point here. I think God just picked him to be my guardian angel that day, to stay with me and keep me calm through all my travails.

It reminded me of the phrase I had heard when I was a child about "Angels Unaware." As defined to me these were people who served in an angelic role without ever being aware of their purpose. Well, Mon was my angel unaware and I thank God he stuck with me through my Atlanta adventure.

Jackie K. Cooper

29

Winning vs. Losing; Winning Wins

You never know what you will do for family and friends. Sometimes you will even surprise yourself. For example, I have never been a sports enthusiast. The exception has been when my children have been playing sports, then I faithfully go to the games and cheer them on. That's what fathers do.

This past summer, however, I became more aware of sports than ever before. For starting in June of this year, my son J. J. covered sports for *The Atlanta Journal/Constitution*. He is a journalism major at the University of Georgia and this was where he served his summer internship.

Several people have told me I must have pushed him into writing since I have a writing career of sorts. That is not true. It is something he decided upon when he was fourteen and started covering sports for *The Houston Home Journal*. From the first article he wrote, he was hooked. And he has stayed hooked all these years.

The first day after he started at the *Constitution* he called me and told me to be sure to get the next day's paper. When I asked why, he answered that he thought he would have an article in it. "I don't think so," was my reply.

Then I told him to let me know what the story was about, just in case they did run part of it. He said I would know it was his because it would have his by-line with it. "I don't think so," I answered again. Well, he did have an article the next day and it did have his by-line, and it was the first of many, many articles he wrote that ran.

Has he exceeded my writing career—Yes! Am I happy about that—Yes! I have always wanted my children to do more than I do. I want them to have it all. So seeing J. J. have this kind of success so early on is pure pleasure to me. And in the process I have learned more about every sports team in Atlanta than I have ever known previously.

Then there is my youngest son, Sean. He is a senior in high school this year. Last year he played football for the first time. Since

Half Way Home

I was not a high school athlete I certainly wasn't pushing him to play. But he wanted to, and that was fine, and he did. However, by the season's end he was ready for it all to be over. "Don't ever let me do this again," he said. "No matter what I say, don't let me get into this again."

Senior year came and football practice time came and no word was said. But a note was left on the refrigerator door saying "I am lifting weights at school." That was the first clue. Later we got confirmation that he was playing again. I didn't say anything—didn't remind him of his vow from the previous year. When you are that age absolutes tend to be forgotten in a day or two.

So the season started. He is playing offense and defense. His mother and I watch and hope and pray he doesn't get hurt. The first two games were disappointing. His school lost both of them. I think Sean began to think of his vow from last year. It just wasn't as much fun as he had hoped it would be.

But last Friday night they won. It was wonderful. You have never heard such whooping and hollering as we parents did. And the attitude of the players was changed overnight. They had won! All that work had been validated!

Parents tell their children over and over, "It's not whether you win or lose, but how you play the game." I heard it all my life and it is still being passed down generation to generation. But believe me there is a lot to be said for winning. Whether it be a ballgame or just a small occurrence in life, we all need to win some time.

With this sports thing, I have seen winning and I have seen losing. Believe me, it is more fun to be part of the winning.

Don't Call Me, I'll Call You

Whenever I grow short-tempered or impatient I recall that my mother raised me to be a Southern gentleman, or better yet, a gentle Southern man. I have always tried to live up to the standards she established. Even at my age I still say "yes, sir" and "yes, ma'am" to most people. And I always try to say "thank you!" for any small favor delivered.

But there is an occurrence in my life that is wearing my manners thin. Fifty years of being well bred is coming to an end. And the reason: telephone solicitations! When and how did this get to be an everyday event in the world of the living? The dead presumably are not so bothered, but with a dedicated phone solicitor, nothing is for certain.

When they first started calling my house I was my usual charming self. My wife told me to say, "No, thank you," and hang up. But I just couldn't do it. I would listen to all they had to say and then decline gently but firmly. Or maybe not so firmly in some instances.

The call that asked for money to take sick kids to the fair always got to me. Year after year I got that pitch and I kept responding 'til that event played out. But last week I got a call asking if I would sponsor sending a sick kid to the movies. They certainly know how to hit home with me.

One night I actually found myself listening to a ten-minute tape on aluminum siding. There was no human on the other end of the phone, just a voice on a tape making its pitch. That was when I woke up and realized I had to get a grip.

So now when they call and start, I immediately say that I don't want any. That usually stops them. But recently I had a guy ask me why not. I mean he challenged me to prove to him I did not need his product. Now why should I have to prove anything? I didn't call him.

So don't call me on the phone asking me to buy anything. I am automatically going to say "No!" Anyway, right now I am into trying to win some kind of sweepstakes. Believe it or not, I am in the finals for at least four of these cash bonanzas. Old Ed McMahon is going to park himself outside my door any minute now.

I do have to ask though; do you think you can really win if you don't send in a subscription? I subscribed at levels one and two, but I had run out of things to order by the time I was a finalist at level three. I hated to blow my big chance right here at the end, so on the envelope where you are supposed to put your sticker if you are ordering something, I left it blank. I figure if they don't know they might just plop it over into the winning stack out of curiosity.

For one contest I ended up ordering some perfume. It was name-brand stuff and I thought I would score some points with my wife by being so generous. It came to the house and she wouldn't put it on. She swears Elizabeth Taylor's "Passion" never smelled like this. Me, I can't tell the difference.

I am sure it is in the cards for me to win in the near future. How do I know? Well, this lady called the house and offered a year's subscription to *Horoscopes Unlimited*. I just couldn't be rude and now I find I am going to have a very exciting October. It has to be the sweepstakes win!

Doogie Howser, Jr.

You are going to have a hard time believing this but when I was in high school I made the decision to study law based on watching "Perry Mason" on television. Some of my classmates watched "Dr. Kildaire" and decided on medicine. Well, at least it seems that way because some of those guys who ended up being doctors certainly didn't seem to have the calling when we were in school.

Now I have never had to go to one of them for medical treatment and it is just as well, it would be hard to offer them the respect necessary in the doctor/patient relationship.

I have a great doctor. He is older than I am (a situation that is getting more and more difficult to find) and he is very serious. We don't laugh and joke at all. It is strictly business from the minute I enter the office until I leave. I like it that way. It gives me confidence.

A few days ago I went for my yearly physical. I had cut back on my food for a few days and thought it would be a good time to rush through the cholesterol tests. As a matter of fact, I fasted for an entire day before the appointment. I went feeling lighter, but with such a headache.

When I got there my good doctor came in and said he had a medical student who was observing with him and wanted to know if it would be all right for him to come in for my physical. Being a good-natured person, I said ok. This was how I happened to meet Doogie Howser's younger brother. You know who "Doogie Howser" is, don't you? He is that kid in the sitcom of the same name. In the show he is only fourteen or so and has a medical degree

His name wasn't really Howser, but he did look younger than springtime and all the other three seasons combined. When he spoke, his voice still hadn't changed. It came out in a croak and a squeak.

My doctor examined my ear and then asked the kid to take a look. Paranoid as I am, I thought he had found some growth in there that shouldn't have been there. Anyway, the kid got out his ear examining equipment and started trying to get it in my ear. He almost punched several holes in my head. He just couldn't get it right.

"Didn't they teach you how to do this in med school"? asked my doctor.

"Yes," he squeaked. "I am just nervous doing this on a live patient."

Finally he got it in my ear and told my doctor he didn't see anything. "Fine," my doctor answered. "I didn't see anything either. I just wanted to see how you held the instrument when you examined the ear."

He then began to take my pulse. When he got to my right foot he told the youngster to give it a try. Determined to be more accurate this time, the kid squeezed my foot with all the pressure he could muster. I let out a yell and the doctor reprimanded him: "Don't kill him, just gently feel the pulse."

By now my foot was pulsating with pain. But the kid had proved his point. I did have a pulse.

As the examination went on and on the doctor would do the test and then Mr. Would-Be-Doctor would do it again. I was getting nervous. There are some tests that should be done only once. Luckily, it was. I am good-natured, but not that good-natured.

Some day this young doctor-in-training will be a serious, grown-up doctor. His patients will have nothing but confidence in him and treat him with respect. But on this day with me, he was all thumbs and all apologies. Still you have to start somewhere.

Go get 'em, doc.

Picking a Cause

Now that the election is over, we have a new president and a lottery. I am going to keep my opinion of President Clinton to myself, but I will say a few words about the lottery. I don't want to get on my soapbox for being for or against it, but I do have some thoughts about the controversy surrounding it. Back when I was in grammar school my brother went to a Halloween carnival at the armory in our hometown of Clinton. He was sixteen or so and went with a friend. The friend for some reason paid his way into the "carnival."

With each ticket of purchase you got a chance to win a washing machine. Why a washing machine, you may ask. I don't know. Maybe the local appliance store gave it as a gift to be raffled off. Anyway a washing machine was the prize and each ticket gave you a chance to win it.

When they entered the carnival my brother handed his friend his ticket stub, but the friend refused it, saying he didn't believe in raffles so he didn't want it. So my brother kept the stub. And wouldn't you know it: when the winning number was read out, it was the one on his ticket.

Before he had a chance to claim the prize, the "friend" demanded the ticket saying that since he paid for it, it was his. My brother being a more agreeable soul than I gave it to him. But it ruined the friendship. And it made me furious. I was at the age when I just couldn't stand that kind of hypocrisy. Come to think of it, I am still at that age.

There are some people who loudly stated their opposition to the lottery. They called it a heinous sin and a crime against God. They made it sound like lightning would strike you dead if you purchased one of those sinful "chances." And on and on they went.

I am convinced those people are like my brother's "friend." If someone gave them a winning ticket, they would break records getting to the place to cash it in. Maybe they would then donate the funds for the good of humanity. I doubt it, but it's a thought.

Half Way Home

Now I plan to buy lottery tickets when they are offered. I have bought them in Florida and I would really prefer that money be used here rather than there. So knowing I planned to buy lottery tickets when they are offered, I voted for the lottery. Let me quickly add this was not a position taken by all members of my family.

It was also not a position supported by many churches and church members. I have heard it said by some that you could not be a Christian and vote for the lottery. I disagree with that position vehemently. I think what is right and wrong on that matter is between you and God. Anything said by humans on that point is pure speculation. It did amaze me that the churches in our area became so aggressive on the matter. I was amazed, stunned, but also pleased. Pleased that our churches could get so stirred up about something. For too long we have become placid in our positions about anything.

Still with so much hunger in our world, with so much violence in our lives, with so much cruelty in our daily living, I would have thought the churches would pick a more substantive issue to get riled up about. Sure the prospect of legalized gambling is an issue but on my list of priorities it is down a ways. It certainly is behind the problem of the homeless, the starving peoples of the world, and the cruelty of people to each other be it through racial prejudices or criminal assaults.

Wouldn't it be great if we saw just as much concern and passion by our church people against the problem of hunger in Middle Georgia? There are people in our area who are suffering, you know. They don't have to worry about the lottery because they don't have any money to spend on it. They are too concerned about making it from one day to the next. The cost of waging the war against the lottery could have fed some of the hungry and homeless for days, months, or even a year.

If you worked against the lottery, that is your business. But if you are going to aggressively fight the ills of the world, I hope you will now pick another issue and pursue it as vigorously as you did this one. Hunger, homelessness, racial bigotry, or others may not be as "safe" an issue as the lottery, but they are much more important.

All of this is just my opinion, but I hope it will give you some food for thought.

Lost and Found

There is a new Macauly Culkin movie out titled *Home Alone 2: Lost in New York.* It is a fanciful adventure about a ten-year-old boy getting lost in the city of New York and having a great time. So much for the magic of the movies. Getting lost is never fun for the lost child or the parent of the child who is lost.

I can only remember being lost once in my life. It happened when I was six or seven. My family and I were visiting relatives in Gadsden, Alabama. My brother, who is three and a half years older than I, had gone with some of my cousins to see a movie—a gorilla movie. Being younger, I was kept at home, but my uncle did say I could ride with him when he went to pick them up.

When we got to the theater my uncle left me at the top of the aisle while he went to look for my brother and cousins. Only a few seconds after he left me, the gorilla came on the screen. That's all it took. One look at that hairy beast and I was out of there.

When I say "out of there," I mean out of there. I ran out of the theater and down the street. I had no idea where I was going, but I knew that gorilla was in that theater so I had best put as much distance between me and him as I could.

I don't know how many blocks I covered, but unlike Macauly Culkin I didn't think it was a lot of fun to be out on the streets alone. I wanted to get to my mother and have the safety and comfort of familiar surroundings. The only problem was that I didn't know how to find them.

Luckily for me a police car passed by and saw this tear streaked child running down the streets and thought they had better check it out. They flagged me down and soon I was in the car with them. The only problem was I couldn't tell them who I was.

It wasn't that I didn't know my name, address, and phone number; it was just that I couldn't talk plainly. For years the only person who could really understand me was my brother. My friends and relatives always looked to him to translate when they couldn't grasp what I was saying.

So when the police asked for my name it came out something like "Aateee Ersaw Ooper." In plain English that is "Jackie Kershaw Cooper," but they couldn't quite make out the wording. Unable to make contact with my parents, they decided to just keep me at the station until somebody called and asked for me. In the meantime they gave me all the candy I wanted—just like in the movies. It didn't take long for my parents to call the police and report me missing and when they did they found a tongue-tied little boy at the station house. In only a matter of minutes we all were reunited. My folks didn't even get mad at me for running out of the theater. They saved all their energy to blast my uncle for leaving me.

In the movie you see Macauly racing around the streets of New York, and he looks like he couldn't be happier. Don't bet on it. Getting lost is no laughing matter. In my case it ended happily ever after, but unlike in the movies, that is not always the case. I have always been fearful my boys were going to get lost or worse yet be kidnapped. When my boys were small I was a basket case whenever they were "misplaced," which wasn't often. Oh, we had some can't-be-found-in-the-store experiences, but only once did we have a full-blown panic attack due to having *lost* a child.

It happened shortly after we moved back to Middle Georgia from our stay in California. We had been out there for a couple of years and had returned home, much to the relief of my wife and children. We had kept our house in Perry while we were away but had rented it out. Now that we were back we had to give the renters notice before we could move back into it.

While we were waiting, we took an apartment in Warner Robins. It was in the same apartment complex where Terry and I had lived when we were first married, so we felt right at home there. And so did the boys. They were eight and five and loved having a playground nearby and a swimming pool to boot.

We never let the children go anywhere by themselves. They were and still are so special that we just knew the evil kidnappers of the world were just waiting to snatch them up and sell them to childless families. So they were only allowed to play in the front of the apartment and only then when they were both together.

One Sunday afternoon Sean pitched a fit to go out and play, but J. J. wanted to watch a ballgame on television, so we told Sean "no." He was furious. Being five meant he always was at the whim of the rest of us. He couldn't make any rules; he just had to abide by ours. And all the crying and begging and persuading he used with J. J. met with no results. He was trapped in the house.

About forty minutes after his last outburst I went into the boys' room and asked where Sean was. "I don't know," said J. J. "I thought he was with you." He wasn't with Terry and me. He hadn't been with Terry and me. We thought he was in with J. J.

Immediately we began to search the house, calling his name. No results. We couldn't find him anywhere. We couldn't imagine he could have gotten out of the house by himself, but it was possible. So we began to search the yard. Up and down the apartment complex we ran, shouting his name, asking any and everyone if they had seen a blue-eyed, blond-haired five-year-old boy named Sean. No one had.

The next step was to call the police. We aren't ones to hesitate about doing that, especially if it concerns our children. But just as I picked up the phone to call I heard a noise. It was something like a sigh or a snore. I listened. It was a snore, and it was coming from beneath Sean's bed.

Hardly daring to breathe, I lifted the spread and looked, and there he was—curled up and sound asleep with his big stuffed raccoon named "Rockella." He had had so many toys and animals gathered around him that we hadn't seen him when we had looked under there before. But there he was.

I never have thought Sean hid under there on purpose. And I don't think he really meant to scare us. First, he has always liked tight places like that. Secondly, when there is nothing else to do he has always been able to go to sleep. So I think he got bored and decided to take a nap under the bed. I still recall that feeling of complete happiness at his being found. Those had been the longest ten or fifteen minutes of my life, and Sean had slept through it all. My "lost lamb" hadn't been lost at all; he was just taking a rest to avoid being bored.

Christmas

Christmas has virtually arrived but you couldn't prove it by me. I haven't felt it in the air or seen it in the faces of the people I have passed on the streets. That doesn't mean people haven't been pleasant, they just haven't seemed to be in the mood.

My own family has been so caught up in final exams and last minute work projects that we haven't had the chance to wonder about the season. But there are still a few days left, so maybe the magic of Christmas will get to us yet.

What worries me most is the feeling some people have that Christmas spirits can be found in a bottle. Too, too often in the past few days or weeks I have heard about a violent car wreck that has left another person dead, and the reason for the seasonal crash was a drunk driver.

Alcohol has been around forever or at least it seems that way to me. I know that when I was a teen—back in the dark, dark ages—I was confronted with the question of to drink or not to drink. I chose not to, but a lot of my closest friends chose to. And I don't think I ever said a thing to any one of them about not doing it. I figured it was their business and not mine.

Then when I was in the Air Force, my wife and I became friends with a couple named Doug and Donna. They were a lot of fun and we enjoyed doing things with them. Doug and I worked in the same office and he was great to help me with things and I would him. He was a great guy, but he was also a guy who drank constantly once he was off work.

From the time he got home 'til the time he went to bed, Doug had a drink in his hand. But he never acted drunk. Well, almost never. He was generally fun, polite, sarcastic, and charming. He had a quick wit and a razor sharp mind he used when talking politics, the military, or life in general.

His drinking was never a problem to us although Donna used to complain about it to Terry sometimes. It was basically live and let live, until the time arrived that we went to a party with Doug and Donna. I usually drove when we went out, but for some reason Doug insisted on driving that night.

Going there he did fine, but after a long night of drinking, he was in no shape to drive us home. We three thought he wasn't, but he insisted he was. And he did drive. He drove like an idiot and jeopardized my life and the lives of our two wives who were in the car with us. It also put in peril the lives of any and everyone who was on the streets of Warner Robins that night.

Oh, we made it home safely, but that is not the point. The point is that by staying silent, the three of us agreed to what he was doing, and that was wrong. Friendship doesn't require that you do that. Friendship requires that you speak up and speak out.

After that night we continued to see Doug and Donna, but we never got in a car with him driving again. Luckily, he never pushed the issue because it might have ended the friendship then and there. And maybe it should have anyway. Because Doug continued to drink and eventually he lost his family and his career because of it. Everybody who cared about him stayed silent until it was just too much. Then they left.

I wasn't a good friend to Doug by staying silent, and I am not a good friend to anyone today by not saying they have had too much to drink. I am more inclined to speak out these days—friendship or not. I hope you are too.

Friendship and love are not proven by saying it's ok to drink and drive. Kids need to tell each other it is wrong even if it makes them unpopular. That is sometimes the price of being in the right.

In the "spirit" of the season let's remember the reason we are celebrating. It is the birthday of Jesus Christ and we are all invited to his party. He isn't serving alcohol.

Christmas is a happy and joyous time. It should also be a sober one. We owe that to ourselves, our families, and all the strangers we might meet on the streets.

Half Way Home

CHAPTER 2

REFLECTIONS FROM ROUTE 93

New Year's Resolutions

The other day I came across a paper my son had written concerning New Year's resolutions. I think it was an assigned paper because I can't imagine J. J. just sitting down and writing things like that out without a reason or requirement.

In this paper J. J. stated his resolution was to lose weight during the coming year. Now on the surface that sounds like an innocuous decision, but when you look at it a little harder you begin to see the trouble it could indicate.

J. J. is a typical twenty-year-old who loves junk food. When he was in high school he could eat it with gusto and never gain a pound. But when he started college his metabolism changed as did his activity and he gained a few pounds. No big thing. He was always a little thin to my way of thinking so I thought the extra pounds looked good on him.

But when J. J. came home and saw some people, they commented on this weight gain. And enough people made the comment that he took it to heart. That is when he began to watch what he ate and started counting calories and fat content. All of this is fine as long as he does not fall into the cycle of thinking anything he eats is wrong for him. I speak from experience when I say the dieting syndrome can drive you nuts. I have been on and off various diets for years—mostly off. And I have felt guilty about my weight for that long.

When I was in high school I was the perfect weight. I could eat anything and I never gained nor lost an ounce. In college I may have put on five pounds at the most. Then I hit law school. I lived with my aunt and uncle and they fed me constantly. They loved to play bridge and snack, so I played a lot of bridge and ate a lot of snacks. My metabolism, well, forget it. It was like someone added water to the recipe and produced the marshmallow man.

By the time I graduated from law school I had added thirty-plus pounds. And I felt like Porky Pig personified. Luckily I went from law school into the Air Force where I was put on a regular system of exercise.

Now I have never been into exercise. I had the body I had as a gift from God, not from any effort I put into it. So the exercise was drudgery for me, but I didn't have any choice. I exercised every day with pushups, sit-ups, and running. This was all done in San Antonio, Texas, where it is hot. Did I lose weight? Did I ever! By the time I finished OTS (Officers Training School) I looked like a refugee from Dachau. I had lost thirty plus another thirty.

It didn't take long after getting away from the exercise regimen for me to start to gain it back. And of course everyone started warning me about getting fat. And warning me about getting fat. And warning me about getting fat!

There isn't a day that goes by that I don't think about my weight. I don't think there is a day that goes by that every single person in America doesn't think about their weight. It is the national pastime and the national obsession. I think about it as I am toting my overfilled plate through the line at the local buffet.

If we are concerned about our weight from a health standpoint that is one thing, but if we are concerned because we think we ought to be slim and look good, that is another.

Life is too short to bother with whether we are as slender as the next person. There are much more important things to worry about. That's why I hope J. J. changes his New Year's resolution and gets off the diet phobia. Just staying the great person that he is, is much more important—for him and for all of us

Stand by Your Child

Being a country music fan I listen to the stations that play this kind of music. And every once in a while I will smile as I hear Tammy Wynette singing "D-I-V-O-R-C-E" and "Stand by Your Man." Well, I think there should be a little variation on the combination of those two songs in real life. In case of "d-i-v-o-r-c-e" you should "stand by your child."

In today's world there is divorce every time you turn around, and in most of those cases the dissolution of the marriage is not a pretty sight. Couples who have at one time been blissfully happy now become antagonistically angry. The wedding vow of "I do" becomes "I will" as in the phrase of "I will get back at you in any way I can."

Recently I have seen two friends' marriages end in divorce. In both instances there have been children involved.

In the case of Burt and Diane there were two children involved—a boy and a girl. Now Burt had always left most of the child rearing to Diane. He provided the money and she provided the care. Now he wants that same arrangement to continue. He thinks that is all that is required of him.

Diane wants the children to have a father who is more active in their lives. She demands that they have a father who is more active in their lives. And since Burt is not being that father she wants him to be, she has decided to punish him by hauling him into court for the least infraction of the divorce decree.

If he doesn't make his child support payments as quickly as she thinks he should, they are fighting through their lawyers. If he doesn't pick the children up and return them as promptly as she thinks he should, they are fighting through their lawyers.

And who is getting hurt most by all of this? Not Burt and Diane. I think they enjoy the bickering to a certain extent. I know they enjoy their small victories of getting the best of each other. But the kids don't. They love both their parents and are being torn apart by their parents' inability to get along.

The other case involved Richard and Dorothy. Richard has always been a real hands-on parent. He and Dorothy's little boy is the apple of his eye. He wants to be with him as often as he can and begs to see him in excess of what the divorce decree allows. But Dorothy is a bitter woman and she uses the little boy as a weapon to punish Richard for leaving her.

Richard has a temper, and it flares up from time to time, but he tries to hold it in check. He knows Dorothy has the upper hand in this situation and can make his life miserable by withholding his son from him. So he tries to get along with her in order to be able to see his child.

Who is being hurt by Richard and Dorothy's fighting? Their son, of course. He sees the two people he loves most in the world constantly arguing. And he is being deprived of his father's influence in his life due to his mother's bitterness.

Now you can say I don't know what I am talking about since I am not divorced. That's true and I hope I never am. But it doesn't take a genius to observe that nine times out of ten warring parties in a divorce case are not thinking about their children when they are fighting. They are playing "hurt the other" not "help the children."

Some day we will see the results of this scarring of our children through the divorce wars. And when we find them as flawed adults it will be too late to undo what we have done. So for their sakes now and for their sakes in the future, when it comes to d-i-v-o-r-c-e, stand by your children and do what is best for them.

ILLNESS IS A PART OF LIFE

Just like clockwork, every New Year's Eve my wife asks me what I want to happen in the upcoming year. Usually I answer with some trivial response such as "sell a story to Hollywood" or "win the lottery." But this year I answered by saying I wanted 1993 to get over with quickly.

It just isn't starting out as a great year. My first cousin was diagnosed with prostate cancer and just underwent surgery and radiation treatment. A week after my cousin was diagnosed, my brother called to say he has prostate cancer. He had surgery last week. Then, in the middle of all this, my father called and said they had discovered he has diabetes. Need I say more?

Luckily my cousin and brother are both doing good and their prognoses are for complete recoveries. As for my father, well, his diabetes can be controlled by diet. No shots or medicine are required at this time. But for a Cooper to have to change his eating habits is a trauma and a half.

I became aware of how upset he was when my stepmother called me at work to tell me he had been diagnosed as diabetic. "You have to talk to him," she said. "He is really depressed."

"Put him on the phone," I said, "and I will see what I can do." My brother never gets phone calls like this. He always gets the happy calls. The ones that say everything is great and we are all happy. I guess there is one child in every family who gets to handle the bad news and I am it.

Anyway, my father got on the phone and began to moan and complain. "I don't guess I will be able to come to Sean's graduation now," he said. "I can't go anywhere 'cause I can't eat regular food any more. I'll just have to say here in this house forever and let Florence (my stepmother) fix me special food."

I tried to explain to him that there were many, many different kinds of foods he could still eat. He didn't want to hear it. "I can't drink Pepsi and I can't eat ice cream," he said. "And I can't ever have any more sweets." I kept on talking, saying how great I had discovered diet drinks to be and how he would learn to love "Sweet and Low." But he wasn't buying it. He just wanted to wallow in feeling bad and not have somebody cheer him up. So I gave him his time of pity. And the more he talked about how bad it was going to be the more he seemed to be cheering up. As a matter of fact, before he hung up he said he felt pretty good.

In typical Daddy fashion, I got a call from him on Saturday, and he said he had decided it wasn't going to be too bad. He had discovered a lot of foods he could have, and even though he couldn't eat as much as he once did, he still could enjoy food.

My father is resilient. Even though he has his down days, he still bounces back. I admire that about him. He told me in that last conversation that it was amazing what doctors can do for you these days. He says as long as they can get it diagnosed they can treat it, and I guess to a large extent that is true.

Nobody likes to get old, and nobody likes to get sick. That is a given. But as we do have problems, it is nice if we can meet them with an optimistic spirit. My father is doing that. So is my cousin. My brother, well, that is a different story. He whines just to hear the sound of his voice whining. Some people are like that too.

No, a lot of people are like that too.

Tomorrow

I read an article in the newspaper the other day about a small town where there had been a particularly violent crime. What amazed me in the story was that several of the residents of the town said that they had never locked their doors before, but now they would. It is hard for me to believe there is any place in this country where people don't lock their doors.

My house stays locked twenty-four hours a day. I don't carry out the garbage without locking the door behind me. I don't think I am necessarily phobic. I think I am just cautious. Still, I do hate the fact that I don't feel safe enough anymore to leave the doors unlocked at any time. That is a price I pay for my modern day life, a price I do not like.

In "the good old days" I didn't have to live behind a mass of locks. There, I've said the phrase, so I guess I am over the hill as far as youth is concerned. I have become my parents. The transition is complete.

So many, many times I have heard my father, or others of his generation, talk about when they were younger or less specifically "the good old days." These times had a golden glow about them that made their young years appear to have been lived in the Land of Oz. I didn't take any of it seriously. I had read history books and knew what those times were like. And it wasn't all great.

But with the years have come the knowledge that some of their old times were not so great too. There were parts of my childhood times that are better than the times we live in now. Not all, but some.

In my early life we did not have our doors locked all the time. I ran in and out of my house with complete freedom and so did my friends. Our neighborhood was one big open house. And this pretty much lasted until the families went to bed at night.

We also were free to move about in my town with less caution. My brother and I walked up town to the movies and back without my parents ever worrying about us being murdered on the way there or back. Those were just not common concerns in those days. It was a kinder, gentler time for us all.

I mourn over this loss of innocence for us and our country. And I wonder if the children growing up today will look back on the 1990s as "the good old days." Is it possible that they will have the ability to say they remember a kinder, more gentle time when the world was not angry and hostile and fraught with dangers?

Maybe they will. I certainly hope they can. I hope and pray and dream and wish that more sanity will come back to our lives. I guess I was infected with the "Annie Warbucks" syndrome at an early age and have the hope of "tomorrow" always in my heart.

The possibility that tomorrow will bring a better day and a better way of life for my children and their children is what makes life worth living. If I couldn't dream about that, well, it would be a bitter way to live. But while we are all dreaming about the good old days, we need to be insuring there will be the same type of days for our children to cherish.

It really isn't possible to hope that sometime in all our tomorrows the locks could come off the doors. If the good old days existed once for us, they can certainly exist again for our children. Tomorrow!

Half Way Home

Take Care of Your Feet

My folks counsel me constantly to take care of my feet. They tell me, based on their own experience, that foot problems are nothing to laugh at. And I know that nothing hurts like bad feet. You have to stand on them. You have to use them to walk. You can't stay off them all the time. So when my feet started hurting I knew I had to make a quick visit to my good old pal Dr. Bunion.

Dr. Bunion was the doctor who cut out my ingrown toenail with zero pain. That is the kind of doctor I like—painless. So now that my feet were hurting and my ankles were swelling I headed straight for his office. The swelling in my ankles had caused me more concern than the pain. That is because I am a total hypochondriac. A few months ago my friend Chuck had been hospitalized with fluid around his heart. One of the first symptoms he had was "swelling in the ankles." "So, watch your ankles, Jackie," he said, and I did. Now they were swollen and I felt a few twinges in my heart.

When I was ushered into Dr. Bunion's examining room the nurse told me to remove my shoes and socks. I did. So my feet were bare and exposed when Dr. Bunion entered the room. "My gosh, they are swollen!" He exclaimed. When I came to, we talked about what could be causing them to swell. He said it could be my heart. It could be my kidneys. It could be diabetes. Or it could be none of the above. In my mind I was thinking, could it be because I am fat?

The first thing he did was order X-rays of my feet. Now there's a silly feeling. You are told to stand on a tray and make sure your toes are flat. My toes always curl so I had to press down as hard as I could to make sure the little piggies didn't look like rolled sausages.

The X-rays showed that I had no chips, cracks, or broken bones. So that left blood work. That's always a fun thing for me since I have collapsible veins and they tend to spurt out blood rather than letting it run out. The lady taking the blood did a good job. She only had to plunge the needle in a few times before she hit pay dirt.

Jackie K. Cooper

The blood tests came back normal also. I was disgustingly healthy. But what about my ankles and my feet? Well, the wise Dr. Bunion decided a shot of cortisone in each foot might be the next best thing to do. As I was waiting to go into his office to get the shots I told various people about the upcoming injections. You can imagine the looks I got. People's faces actually contorted. "Those shots are horrible," they screamed. "Keep the pain. Cortisone shots are worse than anything you are feeling now." Feeling totally insecure, and my faith in the good Dr. Bunion wavering, I made my way to his office with trepidation. Once there, his assistant made the preparations on my feet for the shots. The injections were going to go into the side of my feet. Yuck! Double yuck!

Since the assistant was preparing the needle, I asked her if she was going to do the shots. "She has to learn sometime," yelled Dr. Bunion from the next room.

What a kidder he is. He did the shots himself, and believe me, I didn't even know when he did them. Is this guy a genius or what? My feet are slowly un-swelling and the pain is gone. I haven't been back for another visit yet, so I haven't had to have the good doctor tell me my feet are just fat and flat. But I think that is where we are headed.

Half Way Home

A Look Backward

Last week a group of my college classmates sat down and had dinner together in South Carolina. My college class was holding a reunion. The invitations had been sent out about the activities planned. But I wasn't there. It's not that I didn't want to meet and greet them. I certainly share the normal curiosity about what has happened in their lives. But I also have an aversion to being with a group of people I now know only in memory.

When we graduated oh so many years ago we all pledged to remain friends forever as college people do. We were a closer-than-usual group since we numbered only 100 or so in the senior class. Our ranks had pretty much stayed the same since we entered Erskine College as wet-behind-the-ears freshmen. After college I did stay in touch with a few of these people, especially those who had made the trip to college with me from my hometown of Clinton, South Carolina. But the others began to be scattered like the wind to the far corners of the country. The glue of college life had become undone.

Later I did make one trip back for a reunion. I think it was the tenth. I had just gotten married and I wanted to show my wife where I had gone to college. I also wanted her to meet some of the people I had talked about when recounting my college adventures. She had heard endless stories about the wonderful members of my group and she expected to find dashing and handsome young men and beautiful and brilliant women. That's what she expected. That's not what she found.

My friends, like I, had grown older and had become more rooted to the earth. We were not carefree young boys and girls any more but rather men and women faced with building careers and creating lasting relationships. All those days of solving the problems of the world had been replaced by more immediate needs and situations.

I resolved at that point I would not go back again. Thomas Wolfe had been right—to a point.

Jackie K. Cooper

The people who assembled that Friday night in April are good people. They have made successes of their lives and created a better world just by being in it. But they are strangers to me now. I know of them, but I do no know them.

Still on 2 April, I raised my glass in a toast to all those wonderful young people who shared four years of my life. Four intense years of such beauty and experience that they can never again be recaptured. Four years filled with the highest of highs and the lowest of lows; a time of romance and revelation when our senses were at their most sensitive.

The glory days of college have come and gone for me. In my wildest imaginings I cannot conceive of my ever returning as a student to the halls of academe. Once was enough. And in the case of Erskine, once was pretty much perfection.

My life is still interesting enough for me to spend more time looking towards the future than back to the past. But when I do look back to those college years of the 1960s, it is with a smile. A shadowy smile, but a smile nonetheless.

Car Insurance

There is something about car insurance that I just don't understand. Maybe somebody, somewhere can explain it to me. The whole concept of paying for a service that you are afraid to use just blows my mind. But that is the way most people I know feel about their policies.

With so much current attention being paid to health insurance coverage, why isn't someone crying out about the way the car insurance program is run. Or maybe they are and I just don't know it. Somebody clue me in.

What got me started on this is that a friend of mine was involved in an accident of sorts. His car was parked, minding its own business, and a tractor-trailer rolled into it. The car was smushed. I mean it was pulverized. From what my friend told me it was beyond repair. Now that must have been an exaggeration on his part because they later told him it could be repaired. Still take my word for it, the car was in bad shape.

Let me add this was not a new car. It was about eight or nine years old, but it was in good shape. Now its in bad shape and old beyond its years.

The insurance company for the hitter agreed that they had liability to the hittee. Sounds simple, right? Wrong. Let me continue. My friend asked if a rental car was in the deal. Of course, they answered. Just send us the bill when you are through with renting the car. When he complained that he did not have the up front cash to rent a vehicle, the insurance company said it was their policy only to reimburse for expenses, not provide money up front.

Next my friend learned that the company would accept the car being totaled. The amount it would take to "fix" it was more than the car was worth, so they said initially. My friend took this information and went looking for a comparable car. He found one that sold for $3,000. It was in good shape, had about the same number of miles as his old car, and was the same year of make as his had been.

When he presented this to the hitter's insurance company they said they would only pay $2,000 tops. That is what the "bluebook" said his car was worth. But what about comparability between his car and this one, he asked. Doesn't matter, they answered. We just pay what the fair market value of your old car was.

My friend still argued that his car had been minding its business and had gotten hit through no fault of his. It was unfortunate, the insurance company agreed, but $2,000 was still their top offer. They would, however, agree to fix his car. The amount to do that would be $2,900.

My friend tried to argue that if the company was willing to pay $2,900 to repair the car, why shouldn't they give him that much to put on the purchase of a new car? No, they responded. We will either pay fair market value or have your car repaired.

That is where the situation is now. At a standoff. My friend wants the $2,900 cash in hand, but the insurance company is offering only $2,000. The $900 is in never-never land.

I did ask my friend why he was doing all this haggling. Why didn't he just turn it over to his insurance company and let them handle it. He said he had called his insurer when the accident happened, but they told him it would be best for him to deal with the insurance company of the party that hit him.

Now why would they say that? My friend has been paying premiums on this car for years. And I thought part of the contract was for insurance companies to handle the claims if contacted and then try to recoup from the guilty party.

Maybe my friend just has a bad company—and no I am not going to say which one it is—but it seems to me I hear more and more stories like this. It has become the exception rather than the rule.

For more people times are tough. Money is hard earned and easily spent. So all of us should get the value of services we purchase dollar for dollar. In the case of car insurance I have some doubts.

Most people have insurance. They have to have it. But in way too many cases they are afraid to file a claim on their policy for fear the rates will go up. Isn't that stupid! To pay for something you are afraid to use. At least with health insurance when you use it there is no penalty. I don't understand car insurance. I probably never will. It is one of those necessary evils of life that we all complain about but never get fixed. I'll just add it to my list of things to do.

The Routine of Life

Some people get their kicks and enjoyment of life from the unexpected. Not me. I like for things to be routine and normal. It's the way I have always been and the way I think I will always be.

I can't remember a single vacation I have taken when getting back home wasn't more exciting than going on a trip. Last week I went to San Francisco. I spent five days there, staying at the Ritz Carleton. That is living high on the hog and it was nice. But there wasn't a day that went by that I didn't check it off in my mind as being one day less I would be away from home.

Maybe that is why it is hitting me so hard that my youngest child is getting ready to graduate from high school. When J. J. graduated it was traumatic but I at least still had one son at home with me. Now Sean is getting ready to get his high school diploma and I am losing it. I dread, dread, dread the thought of him going off to school in the fall.

I like having my family close around me. I like having them at my table for their meals. And I like having them inside my home—locked up safely—when nighttime comes. I like the routine of hearing about schoolwork and school activities, and all the other mundane things of regular life.

Normalcy appeals to me, as I am a creature of habit. I like to do the same things over and over. I like to see the same people over and over. Some would say I am in a rut but that is not the way I see it. Every Sunday we go to the same restaurant and I have practically the same food. Usually we eat with the same couple and probably have the same conversations over and over. I love it!

On Friday I go to another specific favorite restaurant and eat. I have a friend who accompanies me there. He likes the food. I love the food. I also like knowing the names of the waitresses and seeing some of the same people week after week. That is comforting to me.

Last week "Knots Landing" had its last show and this week "Cheers" bites the dust. Now why do those shows have to end? I have been watching "Knots Landing" for something like fourteen years and

"Cheers" for eleven. I counted on them being on TV forever. But now they are going, going, gone.

At least I can count on my church family staying basically the same. I love going to my Sunday school class and seeing the same people there, some of them sitting in the same seats week after week. Oh, we have new people who come and join us every now and then, but it is a slow absorption and nothing radical.

When I find out that someone is moving away from Perry, I am distraught. Why would they leave, I ask myself. Don't they know how lucky they are to be a part of such a quiet society! It never dawns on me to think that the reason they are leaving is because it is so quiet.

Now I have excitement in my life. When I was in San Francisco I interviewed Michael J. Fox, Don Johnson, and Rebecca DeMornay among others. When I think of the opportunities I have to do things like this, I can hardly believe my luck. But if I had the chance to exchange my routine normal life for one of constant travel and turmoil I would have to say no thanks.

Having a chance to travel and meet people is exciting, but it is the constancy of my wife, my children, my faith, my friends and my work that make my life so enjoyable. If you want to live for the unexpected—have at it! As for me, I will take the routine any day.

Jackie K. Cooper

San Francisco

I visited San Francisco recently and while I didn't leave my heart there, I did leave my heartburn. Yes, during the six days I was there the hills of San Francisco almost did me in. If you have never visited this city you might not know what I mean, but if you have ever set foot on the sidewalks of San Francisco then you definitely know.

It all started when I got an invitation to fly out to the city by the Bay and preview the upcoming Disney Studios summer slate of movies. As bad as I hate to fly, I couldn't turn down this offer. So with two carry-ons in my possession I left Atlanta to fly the friendly skies.

Let me back up a bit before I get too far ahead of myself. When I got to Atlanta I went to the "long term parking area." Each and every time I go there that place is filled to capacity. And each time like an idiot I drive around and around and around hoping/praying/begging for someone to vacate a slot near the front of the lot. No one ever does.

After parking near the back fence I hoofed it to the building. Once on the flight I was dying for a drink. So as soon as it was offered I got a Diet Coke and even boldly asked for the entire can. Well, in actuality the guy next to me asked for a Coke with two glasses of ice. That resulted in him getting the whole can rather than a poured drink. I thought that was pretty smart, so I asked for the same thing.

One thing that amazed me on this flight was that there was nowhere to hang a garment bag. It was either put it in the overhead bins or check it. I never, ever check a bag if I can help it, so into the overhead it went. But when did they stop offering that service? Even a sporadic flyer like myself has always had that convenience.

The flight was rough and bumpy but not unbearable. I keep my seatbelt on at all times anyway unless I am crawling up the aisle to get to the bathroom. On this flight the "fasten seatbelts" sign was on most of the time.

Things smoothed out when we got to California. I even managed to peer out the window and see the bay as we passed over it and into the airport. And after a smooth landing (my compliments to the pilot), I was out of the plane and on my way to the Ritz Carleton.

During the time I was there I got to see *What's Love Got to Do with It? (The Tina Turner Story)*, *The Son-In-Law*, and *Life with Mikey*. I also got to interview Don Johnson, Rebecca DeMornay, Laurence Fishburne, Angela Bassett, and Michael J. Fox among others. (Am I lucky or what?)

One day when I had some free time I decided to walk around the area by the hotel. Someone had said Chinatown was nearby and I thought it might be interesting to see. So off I went.

Believe me on this, you don't walk anywhere in San Francisco without climbing hills. I learned this the hard way. The first street I encountered was flat. The next one was a bit inclined. The next one was a mountain. By the time I reached the top of it my chest was burning and I was gasping for air. Forget Chinatown! Forget anywhere else in San Francisco! I was pooped.

I observed the little cable cars moving by and thought I might catch a ride back on one of them. But they don't stop for passengers. You have to run and jump on. I couldn't have run anywhere in my condition. So I just slowly shuffled back down the hills and back to my room where I collapsed. So much for playing tourist.

That night I was taken to a "Rave Club." Do you know what a "rave" club is? Well I didn't either until I made this trip. While out there the folks at Disney threw a party to celebrate the opening of the movie *Super Mario Brothers* and it was held at a rave club.

Let me give you my definition of what I have perceived a rave club to be. It is a place where the music blares, the strobe lights flicker, and people dance all night long. At least that is what happened at this rave club while I was there.

Entering the club itself was pretty neat because they had it fixed so you went in via a tunnel of sorts. This is in keeping with the theme of *Super Mario Brothers* wherein a tunnel figures into the story line. Once inside the club we were met by a fire-eater. Now what that had to do with the *Super Mario Brothers* I don't know. I didn't see one of those in the movie and I don't think there is one in the Nintendo game. But anyway he was there and eating fire like mad.

The dance floor of the club was open and people were dancing in a frenzy. Not me, I haven't danced since my high school class did the bunny hop. Some people who were out there dancing shouldn't have been. The nice thing about modern dancers though is that they don't care if they have a partner or not. They just get on the floor and start gyrating to the music.

The music was provided by a guy in a booth playing records. And believe it or not most of the songs were out of the 1970s disco craze era. I even heard one by the Bee Gees. Next thing you know people will be dressing up in white suits again and striking John Travolta poses.

For this party there was a buffet table set up in one corner and then there were tables and chairs on a balcony that went three quarters of the way around the club. So you could get your food, watch the dancing, and/or watch the guy eat fire.

In another corner was a bar and in another one was a place where they were dispensing "smart drinks." That was another term with which I was not familiar. I questioned the bartender and he said smart drinks were non-alcoholic concoctions made of fruit juices blended with amino acids and a variety of vitamins. It all comes out as a frothy brew that is supposed to give you enhanced brainpower and energy with which to dance the night away.

Being a brave soul I decided to have a "smart" drink and increase my brainpower. I liked the way it tasted, but I never got the feeling I was any smarter or even any more energetic. So much for smart drinks. I was probably dumb to think it would make any difference.

While I was in San Francisco, I did decide that high priced, fancy food is wasted on me. The night before the "rave" party I went to another celebration. This one was at a restaurant established by Wolfgang Puck, the gourmet chef of all gourmet chefs. Or at least that is what I heard.

Wolfgang is supposedly famous for his special pizzas, and that is what was served at the party. They came in all shapes and sizes but none were your basic beef and onion. That is the kind I like. These babies had snails and different types of fish topping that turned my taster off.

Salmon is also the big dish of choice in California these days. Every buffet table I saw at any of the functions always had a large spread of salmon. There wasn't any country style steak to be seen anywhere. It wasn't until I was on the airplane coming back that I had regular food.

So I guess you can take the man out of Georgia, but you can't take Georgia out of the man. Rave clubs, smart drinks, Puck pizzas, and a lot of salmon just don't make it for me. Oh, its great to have the experience of visiting the clubs and being offered the food, but inside I am always just one step away from the vehicle that takes me home.

The Graduate

A few weeks ago my youngest son graduated from high school. I also celebrated my twenty-third wedding anniversary, plus I had the joys of "Father's Day" once more. Now that is an abundance of events.

By far the most traumatic of these experiences was Sean's graduation. Why oh why, I ask myself, did we stop with two children. What we need now is another one in reserve to fill up our lives when both of the boys are in college. But I guess you can never have enough children. They all grow up and move on with their lives. I just hope they will continue to make us a part of theirs.

The graduation experience itself was a good one. My parents and my in-laws came for the event and joined us and several of our friends for an after-graduation celebration. It was a night like we wanted it to be and I think Sean felt like he graduated with style.

The scariest part of the occasion occurred when my folks and my in-laws left for the Perry Agricultural Center where the graduation ceremonies were to be held. My father has some health problems and it is hard for him to get around easily any more. Since he walks with a cane, I sent them on early to get a good seat on the floor of the auditorium.

When Terry and I got there I couldn't find them. Then I looked up in the bleachers and there they were halfway to the ceiling. When I asked what had happened they said they couldn't see on the floor, so Joe (my father-in-law) got someone to help and they dragged Daddy up to where the two ladies wanted to sit. All four now said they could see fine.

The problem was that all during the ceremony I wondered how we were going to get him down. Daddy is much better going up stairs than coming down them. But luckily we made it out of the Ag Center after the graduation with no problems.

It amazed me how coherent and interesting the speeches by the students were at this graduation. I usually am looking at my watch and wanting it all to be over. This is due to my very short attention span for oratory. But these talks were fun, informative, and enjoyable.

I also noticed there was an empty chair with a white ribbon across it in the middle of the seats for the graduates. At first I thought it was just a seat to separate the girls from the boys but then I realized it was for the classmate of the students who had been killed in an accident when they were in grammar school. It was a wonderful gesture on the part of the students and I know it meant everything to the parents of that child to know he had not been forgotten.

After all the festivities of graduation it was hard to get back into the normal day to day activities. But then it was anniversary time followed by "Father's Day." I made the trek up to Clinton, South Carolina, and took my father out to lunch on the Saturday before the actual "day."

The "day" itself was reserved for my boys. J. J. is up in Athens this summer, so we three went up there and had our time with our total family. Poor Daddy had to make do with celebrating the week before.

My Sunday school teacher was giving the lesson a few weeks ago and mentioned it is harder for him to be a son than it is to be a husband and father. That is so true for me also. Doing the necessary things that are required of a husband and father come easy to me, but when it comes to the "son" things, I have to make an effort.

The awareness of that scares me. I certainly don't want my kids relegating me to a level of importance that is behind other areas of their lives. But it could happen.

I think though that parents today are more involved in their children's lives than mine were. Maybe it is because we were the first generation that actually chose to have children. My father's generation felt more of an obligation to have kids. It was the thing to do. You had them even if you didn't want them. Now I think it is more of a choice thing although there is still societal pressure to reproduce. But there are many people who say no thanks to the option of having children.

Finally, the anniversary was great. My wife and I went to a restaurant in Macon to celebrate. As we were driving up the interstate a car pulled out from the Warner Robins exit and came up beside us. It was a small car, covered with the markings of "Just Married" and various other slogans. The bride was identified as Lori and the groom as James.

They looked so young and eager that it took your breath away. And it was almost surreal having them beaming across at us on our anniversary date.

We rode down the interstate together until the road divided for the turn off to Atlanta. They waved and then they were gone—on their way to start what I hope for them will be a wonderful twenty-three years and more.

Life goes on. Graduations, holidays, and anniversaries—all are part of the cycle of life that goes on and on and on.

Angels Unaware

When I was a very little boy I remember my mother reading me a book called *Angel Unaware*. It was written by Dale Evans Rogers about her daughter, Robin. The book really made an impact on me, and its message has stayed with me all my life.

The whole point of the book was that Robin was an angel sent by God and that she was unaware of it. I really believe that many times I have run into people who were "angels" and didn't know it.

I met another one the other day and her name was Shirley. She didn't have wings, didn't have a halo, and wasn't dressed in white, but I recognized she was an angel just by the way she acted. She was working in the Sears men's department at the Macon Mall.

The day I met Shirley I really needed an angel. I had been trooping around the mall for hours shopping for a birthday present for my father. I wasn't having any luck and I had been scorned and shuttled off by scores of uninterested sales clerks. This had made me terribly hostile. I had no gift to show for my labors and my attitude was that all the salespeople hated their customers.

Then I met Shirley. She was just standing there when I walked into the store. I asked about some key chains and other things and she showed me what was available.

When I told her about shopping for my father's birthday she quickly made a few suggestions, and then as I told why one thing after another wouldn't suit him, she commiserated with me about buying for an elderly relative.

It was as if I had found a kindred spirit who lightened my load by sharing my frustration. Even though I didn't buy anything from her, I felt better for having been around her.

Next I walked over to the shoe department and found a leather bag that I thought might do, since my father is going to make a trip to Canada this fall. I couldn't find a salesperson in this area, so I went back to Shirley. She said since it wasn't her department she couldn't ring it up but that she would find me someone who could.

In a few minutes she was back. She hadn't found me a salesclerk, but she had decided she could ring it on her register. And she did. But then I realized I needed a box to mail it in. No problem, said Shirley, she would find me one.

Now you would think there would be one right where the leather bags were kept, but there wasn't. There were just bags on the shelf sitting loose. But determined, Shirley went foraging somewhere and returned with the perfect box in a few moments.

When I complimented her on her wonderful behavior she responded it was just her job. Just her job? What a fantastic attitude! See why I think she's an angel?

So if you are out shopping any time soon and you are tried, frustrated or out of sorts, just head for Sears and ask for Shirley. Whether you make a purchase or not you will feel better just for having had her wait on you.

And as you are walking away, take a quick look back at her. If she doesn't know you are watching you might just see her halo and wings.

College Bound

I don't want to think about it. I don't want to believe it. Still the time has come and my baby boy is going off to college. I don't know where those eighteen years have gone, but in the blink of an eye they have disappeared. Just like that song that talks about the years flying swiftly by.

Sean has always been special to me, just as my son J. J. has always been special to me—but in different ways. Sean's greatest asset is his personality. He is perpetual sunshine. His face naturally goes to a grin even when it is relaxed. And he genuinely likes people—all people. I can just imagine what a great time he is going to have at college meeting hundreds of different people at one time.

It's going to be tough letting go. Terry and I have tended to baby Sean most of his life, and he was great about letting us do it. Unlike J. J. who drew the line on some of our coddling, Sean has been a good sport about it all.

It hasn't been easy for him. Terry has a tendency to call him "precious" regardless of where we are. So some of his friends began to call him precious too. Can you imagine the embarrassment of that! But he took it with a grin just like everything else.

You know, it is hard to spend eighteen years being a parent and then have the object of that attention move away. I mean it can be gut wrenching, traumatizingly bad for the parent. And to some extent for the child.

I remember when I went off to college my father and my aunt took me to Erskine. It was only thirty-five miles away from home, but that seemed like a far distance to me. I lay in the back seat and slept, which has always been my way of escaping from unpleasantness. Then when we arrived it was like I was being cast adrift in an unknown world.

My only consolation was that now I could smoke openly. I had been sneak smoking for a year or more. Dumb me, I smoked in my bedroom and thought my father didn't know it. I guess I thought the

Jackie K. Cooper

73

smoke smell just evaporated. So here I was alone at college and I could smoke just like the big guys. I remember one of my friend's mothers went home and told people that the first thing she saw when she took her son to Erskine was Jackie Cooper with a cigarette in his mouth. Thanks a lot!

Well, I no longer smoke. I saw the light that it was a bad habit. And I trust that Sean won't start. I don't think he will. I hope he will just be so caught up in a new school and new friends that he won't have any homesickness at all.

As for Terry and me, well last weekend just the two of us rode up to Augusta to see some friends. We first went to a movie, of course, and then went out to dinner with them. We didn't head back until after 11:00 and so we didn't get to our house until 2:00 in the morning. But who cared? It was just us. We didn't have to worry about children being unattended.

That type of freedom is the new phase we are entering. And since we are still each other's best friend, it should be pretty nice. Not as good as having kids at home but still bearable and maybe even enjoyable.

The Music Man

Mr. Francis Nunn died recently. His death will certainly leave a void in the hearts of people in Middle Georgia. He made huge contributions to Perry and all of Houston County, as a civic leader and businessman. He was liked and admired by all.

Mr. Francis took the time to be busy and involved in many different functions, but his heart was always at the Perry United Methodist Church.

The first time I ever visited the Perry Methodist Church I met Mr. Francis. Chip Washington invited me to go with him to church one Sunday night and as fate would have it his Sunday School class was making up the choir for the service. So I tagged along with Chip into the choir loft and joined in.

Months later when Terry and I had moved to Perry and joined the church Mr. Francis, as he was called by one and all, was there to ask me when I was going to join the choir.

Mr. Francis had been the choir director there for many years and he was very persuasive at getting people involved. He just wouldn't take no for an answer. The only person who could manage to stay out of the choir on a regular basis was Mr. Francis's son George.

George's wife, Janet, sang in the choir as did his mother Coralee, but George just made "guest" appearances from time to time—a cantata here and a cantata there. But for the rest of us it was a Sunday ritual.

It seemed to me that Mr. Francis had a lot in common with that band leader in the play *The Music Man* who taught kids to play band instruments by the "think" method. They would just think about the music and then play it.

Well a lot of us singers in that choir sang by the think method but with a little difference. Just because Mr. Francis thought we could, we sang. Not all of us could read music, so we would have Mr. Francis sing our part through and then we would imitate him. Don't knock it, it worked.

Each year the church choir would put on something called the Spring Sing. I think Mr. Francis created this event. Anyway it was something the entire community looked forward to every year.

The first year we were in Perry I kept telling Mr. Francis I would take part in this music marathon, but somehow I didn't make it to practice until just before the date of the sing. I raced into the choir loft, grabbed a book of music, and launched into some familiar hymn. I thought and sang and thought some more.

One religious number after another sprang forth from our mouths and our hearts as we were caught up in the music. Finally Mr. Francis said it was time for a lighter number. He passed out some sheets and when I saw what we were going to sing I almost passed out. The organ boomed, the piano chimed, and forty voices joined together to sing "Oklahoma!"

In my church in South Carolina we would never, ever have thought of singing "Oklahoma!" It just wouldn't have been proper. But somehow because Mr. Francis was directing this choir and selecting this song, it was suddenly the most proper ending to a great night of singing.

That was Mr. Francis. He always had a song in his heart and a tune on his lips. He loved music more than any man I have ever known. And when he was singing God's praises he was at his best.

All of us will miss Mr. Francis but I know in my heart that the angels' choir in heaven was glad to get his tenor voice. And I also know that even now they are all joining in with a rousing chorus of "O-K-L-A-H-O-M-A!"

You Have to Love and Respect Your Car

Remember how in *Gone with the Wind* Prissy declared she didn't know nothing about birthin' babies. Well, I can say the same thing about fixin' cars. My knowledge about how cars operate is minuscule. I am not a person who tinkers on them, takes them apart, knows what makes them go. My knowledge is limited to putting gas and oil in them and turning on the ignition. I am a very basic person.

The first car I ever remember having was a Pontiac. I don't know what year it was, but the floorboard was so corroded that you could see the ground as you were driving. And the glove compartment was held up by a Band-Aid. But who cared. In those days gas was twenty-something cents a gallon and my girlfriend and I could spend an entire Sunday afternoon riding around on one tank of gas.

My next car was the color of a lima bean and looked like one too. I had it when I was in law school and it got me back and forth to class, which was its only obligation. I always talk to my cars when I get them and tell them what I expect. I haven't had one let me down yet.

Which brings me to my latest car story. My wife, Terry, had inherited one of my old cars as her vehicle. It was an Oldsmobile, which is my brand of choice. It also helps that my cousin is an Olds dealer in South Carolina and gives us good deals on trade-ins.

Anyway, Terry's car had 172,000 miles on it. That isn't a typo. It had 172,000 miles on it and proud of them all. The car still rode smoothly, but it did have a dent in its side, and the roof covering was sagging down. Now I have never had a car lose it elasticity in the ceiling like this one did. When you were driving you had this material hovering around your ears.

We finally decided it was time to trade it in for another Olds. I called my cousin and he said if we could get it to Clinton, South Carolina, he would take it as trade in on a new car. Getting it to South Carolina was the kicker.

So last Saturday we started out. We had the car phone with us in case we got stranded and I had alerted my parents, who also live in Clinton, that they may have to come get us.

Terry insisted that she drive. Now this is something out of the ordinary, as Terry never likes to drive. But she thought I would not know how to "handle" her car. I agreed and took my place in the passenger seat. The ceiling material had been pinned up, so it was not encompassing my head. We also had the rearview mirror in the backseat as it had come unstuck and wouldn't hold glue to the mirror.

Saying a quick prayer and patting the car we started off on our 200-mile trip. Everything went fine until we got between Macon and Milledgeville. Then the oil light went on. No big thing. We stopped at a convenience store, bought a quart of oil, and went on. Just outside of Milledgeville, the light came on again.

We pulled over to the side of the road and the light went off. We went five miles and it was back on. Terry panicked. I stayed calm. It is probably just the switch I offered. She, however, insisted we could not drive it with the oil light on or we would burn up the engine.

Using the trusty car phone, she called the mechanic that we use. As I knew, he said he couldn't give much advice about a car going down the road seventy miles away from him. He just said that if the light stayed on we had better pull over.

Terry was now having a quiet breakdown, muttering under her breath about how she knew we should never have started out in a car with 172,000 miles on it. I stayed calm. I trusted the car. And as I replaced Terry behind the wheel, I had faith we would make it.

The rest of the trip went like this. Drive five or ten miles, have the oil light come on, pull over and cut off the motor, start it back up and drive on. We did this for the next 120 miles. Then when we were 10 miles from my cousin's shop, we just said to heck with it and went all out. We made it with everything working just fine and the oil light finally blinking off. As we drove off in our new Olds I could look back and see the old Olds sitting in the car lot. I am sure she will find a new owner. There's still life in her yet. And I hope they know how to treat her with respect, for if they do she will do the same.

Half Way Home

Remembering Christmas

I don't know how you feel about it but this year it seems to me there is something wrong with the most right season of the year. As we get into closer to Christmas I hear too many people saying they want to just get Christmas over and done with and move on. They are afraid of the cost of things this year—too afraid they will overspend—and are depressed by the prospect of it all.

Now what has happened to make so many of us feel that way? We grow up being taught that Christmas is a magical time, a time when we are the happiest. But as we get older the responsibilities of life tend to weigh us down.

Of course, when I was little I was a real pain about Christmas. I would never tell my parents what I wanted Santa to bring me. When I was really small I would tell them that he already knew what I wanted and didn't need a letter. When I got older I entered my "surprise" stage.

The "surprise" stage consisted of my saying I wanted a special surprise for Christmas. I didn't know what it was that I wanted but I knew that I would know if I got it or not. Each year my poor parents tried a variety of different gifts they thought might meet the criteria of surprise and each Christmas I got up, went into the living room and looked at the gifts under the tree, and each year said, "I didn't get my surprise!"

It's a good thing I was not my own parent. I am sure that I would have reacted in a much more negative way than they did. And it is for sure that I would not be as tolerant of my own children as my parents were of me.

But my "surprise" phobia is indicative of what is wrong with all of us today. We want more, more, more! The days of Christmas have become the days of greed. You see people shopping and buying electronic games, television sets, cars, and on and on. Then on the other scale you hear about people who don't even know if they are going to be able to get through the Christmas season with food, clothing, and shelter.

Every year I say I am going to be more sensible in what I buy and give, then each year I get caught up in the give syndrome one more time. That means that I go out and buy just to buy. My wife criticizes me for this all the time and she is right. I wait until the last minute and then just do panic buying.

My parents probably have the right idea. They give each other a check. Of course, this makes absolutely no sense as they have a joint checking/savings account so they are in effect giving each other their own money. But they think it makes sense and so they are happy with it. Who am I to tell them it doesn't make sense. Maybe it is a way of saying to each other that they have permission to spend "X" amount of dollars.

This year I am going to try to get my mind in better shape for Christmas and be more positive. I have already messed up some by not helping get the Christmas tree decorated. But maybe I can actually get gifts for my friends and family that serve a purpose.

When we realize the true reason for the season it is a little idiotic to wish it away. And even when we stop and think why we give gifts to each other it makes griping about spending too much seem petty. We give gifts as a way to say to another person how much they mean to us. So it isn't some exercise in seeing who can spend the most. It truly is the thought that counts.

This Christmas season I am going to sit myself down and have a good talking to—with myself. I am going to lecture myself on the true meaning of the day. I am going to work on getting all the negative out of my mind and go with the right attitude. This way maybe I can relax and enjoy Christmas in the right spirit at this the "most right" time of the year.

The Panic King

Is anybody in your family a worrier? Generally, there is at least one in every family unit, and sometimes two. I am the one in my family. They call me the "panic king" because I have been known to blow even the smallest incident all out of proportion.

The problem I have is that I am a worrier and I have a vivid imagination. That is a deadly combination if there ever was one. Not only do I panic when my wife and/or children are late coming home from some event; I also invent the most insane scenarios of what could have delayed them.

When Terry and I first married it drove her crazy when I would meet her at our front door enraged that she was late. She was a grownup, she said, and could certainly take care of herself. That didn't help me in any way. I still panicked every time she ran a few minutes late. So now she takes the time to call and tell me if she has been delayed. That helps me over the "panic attack."

After our boys were born I didn't have panic attacks over them until they were old enough to start driving. Up until that point we had barely let them out of the house. When your kids grow up being allowed only to ride their bicycles in the house (from room to room) you know you are a bit overprotective.

Here's an example of my type of wild-minded panic. The other night my oldest son J. J. had gone to Atlanta to cover a sports story for the Atlanta Journal/Constitution. He stated before he left that he would be late getting back. Now keep in mind, J. J. is twenty-one and has always been responsible. So responsible that sometimes I think he is older than I am.

Anyway, I didn't expect him back until around midnight. And I didn't know that Terry had told him to call if he was going to run later. So when the phone rang around 11:45 I was surprised. The phone in our house doesn't usually ring after 10:00 unless it is my brother calling for some late night consultation, or one of the boys saying they are running late.

When I answered the phone and said, "Hello," there was dead silence. I tried "hello" again and again and again. Still nothing. Then I heard J. J. asking, "Hello?" I hollered back his name but nothing again. Then the line went dead.

Terry came downstairs a minute later and asked who was on the phone. I told her it was a wrong number. That eased her mind, but mine was beginning to race. Why hadn't J. J. been able to hear me, I wondered? Why had the phone connection stopped so abruptly and when was he going to get home were my next thoughts.

I made my way into the living room and as quietly as I could, dialed his cell phone. No answer. Now my imagination did go into overdrive. I could see the wreck in my mind and J. J. trying to reach the cell phone to ask me to help him. Or I could see the kidnapper sitting in the car with a gun drawn on him, smirking as the phone rang and rang. These and a million other ugly thoughts raced through my mind.

Around 12:30 J. J. called again. He was home and safe in Athens. His cell phone battery had gone dead so he couldn't call from the car. Simple explanation, and one I hadn't considered. I had only concocted the bad scenarios.

Sometimes I wonder why God doesn't give us the information at birth as to when the bad times are going to occur. You know, kind of a "Map of Happiness." It would tell me I would have twenty-five years before any thing really bad happened. Then for all those years you wouldn't have a worry in the world. Right? Wrong!

If I found out nothing bad was going to happen for twenty-five years, I would spend all my time worrying about that twenty-sixth year. It would drive me nuts trying to imagine what bad thing could be coming down the pike.

The way it is now I could never have anything bad happen in my entire life. It isn't likely but it is possible. Once again God is right to do it His way. Any worrying I do is my own fault. The future could be perfect. But then it could also be really bad. Uh-oh, the Panic King is back on the throne.

Experience—The Teacher

We ought to try to learn from each and every experience we go through in life. And now that Christmas has come and gone I am able to look back at it with a clearer head. There are several things I learned from the holiday season of 1993.

Number one is: Don't have your brother and your parents visit at the same time; number two is: don't have your in-laws arrive hours after your parents have left; number three is: don't, for any reason, put off a trip to Jekyll Island in order to stay home and have company.

As you probably guessed, I violated all of those rules this past holiday season. At first I thought my folks would not be coming to my house for Christmas. I thought my in-laws were coming. But their plans were changed and they decided not to come till the day after Christmas, the day my parents were leaving.

When I thought it was to be in-laws for Christmas I called my brother in St. Petersburg and gave him the good news. The folks belong to you this Christmas, I advised. Since we had been host for Cooper gatherings for the past ten years, I didn't feel particularly mean spirited in letting him have his share of being a host.

"What do you want me to do with them?" he asked with a whine in his voice.

"Take them to Hawaii!" I shot back. Now this is a fifty-five-year-old, intelligent man. He knows how to drive a car and chew food.

Even though he is the divorced son in the family, he can still function. But he didn't think so.

"How will I feed them?" he asked next.

"They love fast food," I countered. I wasn't going to let him weasel his way out of this one.

But of course he did. When the in-laws put their plans on hold I reverted back to plan one, which was Christmas at my home. And of course I extended an invitation for my brother to come along for the ride. He agreed.

He got to my house on Friday afternoon at 2:00. This was Christmas Eve. By 3:00, my parents had not gotten there. I became a little worried and decided to call the motel where they had reservations to see if they had checked in yet. They were there and the clerk put me through to their room.

"Oh, we just got here," my stepmother responded: "We will be right over." And they did get to our house in about fifteen minutes.

Shortly after they got there, Daddy said something about their leaving South Carolina at 9:00 that morning. Boy, you should have seen the look my stepmother shot him for that one. "Tom, it wasn't 9:00. It was more like 10:00 or 11:00," she assured me.

"Nope, it was 9:00," maintained Daddy. When he gets something in his head he sticks to it. And he knew he was right about the 9:00 A.M. start time.

I soon figured out that they had left the house at 9:00 and gotten to the motel in Perry a little before 2:00. That is when their favorite soap opera, "Days of Our Lives" is on TV. They ordered a little room service, kicked back and watched their show, and *then* came to my house.

Let me explain why they stay in a motel. I don't want to seem too much like the "Grinch of Christmas past." My father had both his knees operated on and now walks with a cane. He has terrible balance and it is dangerous for him to go up and down stairs. In my home all the bedrooms are on the second story. Therefore, it is easier and safer to stay in a motel.

Also, my stepmother is a very, very, very, very light sleeper. She can hear any noise—any noise—that goes on in a house after 10:00 P.M. (her bedtime). My family doesn't go to bed that early, so she was always being disturbed. That is the second reason for the motel.

Anyway now it is 3:00 P.M. and we are all gathered in the Cooper home on Laurel Street. Terry got out some snacks for everyone to munch on and that is when my brother broke off the cap on one of his front teeth. Christmas was off to a great start!

With his tooth missing, he not only looked like a one-fang vampire; he also tended to have "th's" on the end of his words. For example, "yes" became "yeth," "house" became "houth," etc.

I have to admit he was a pretty good sport about the tooth and didn't panic. He wasn't in pain and said he would have it fixed when he got back to St. Petersburg, Florida where he lives. He still insisted on taking us all out for a Christmas Eve meal. Well, not all of us. My youngest son was over at his girlfriend's house having Christmas Eve with her family.

My oldest son, Terry, my brother, my parents, and I piled into two cars and went to eat. I wanted to go by my church and have communion before we went, but I was voted down. Besides, my church had decided not to have a "drop-in" communion service, opting instead for a full service. Well, just let them try it, I thought, they won't have anybody show up. Shows what I know—they had hundreds.

I guess my preference for a "drop-in" communion service will be on hold during this current preacher's term or I will have to find another church to adopt me for that night.

Anyway we went to the restaurant communion-less. My brother graciously told us to order anything we wanted off the menu. My stepmother ordered an appetizer of soup. I did also. When it came it almost scalded my lips it was so hot. Somehow my stepmother's was not as hot.

"There are two things I want hot," she remarked, "my coffee and my soup."

All throughout the rest of the meal she kept making comments about the soup. Could they have gotten it out of two pots, I wondered? I mean, how could mine have been so hot and hers have been so cold? It didn't matter that the rest of the meal was wonderful, we kept going back to the issue of the soup. I could see steam coming out from my brother's ears.

"Juth forget the thoup," he said. Now there were two things cold—the soup and my stepmother.

The rest of the evening crept by until finally it was time for my folks to go to the motel. My brother drove them over and I picked him up. When we got them settled we made our getaway back to my house.

Jackie K. Cooper

85

The next morning was Christmas and we made it through the present opening with nobody's feathers getting ruffled. Everyone seemed to enjoy their gifts, and everyone liked the breakfast Terry prepared—hot coffee and all.

After we finished breakfast I wondered what I was going to do to entertain everyone. My youngest, Sean, came up with an idea. He produced a deck of cards and suggested he and my brother play my parents in a game of "Setback." Great idea, I thought, but then my brother said he wanted to take a nap, so I ended up as Sean's partner.

We played Setback for four hours while my brother slept and my wife slept. Even Fluff, the cat, slept. But there was no nap for me. I shuffled cards, I dealt cards, I played cards. And Sean was with me every step of the way. God love him, what a good sport!

Finally, it came time to go and visit some friends and have supper with them. My folks left to get changed. My brother woke up and was sociable as could be. He was very rested. And my wife came downstairs from her nap. Everyone was feeling grand but Sean and me. We were like two discards.

While I was getting dressed I heard my parents come back, and I heard my stepmother's voice sounding angry.

The problem was the motel. When my parents got back to their room it had not been touched. The beds had not been made, the bathroom had not been cleaned, there weren't even any fresh towels. No clean-up crew had darkened this door.

Being more aggressive than my father, my stepmother called the front office and asked what had happened. "It's Christmas Day," she was told. "We don't have a clean-up crew on Christmas Day."

After much argument the manager did agree to bring some clean towels—if they really needed them.

My stepmother's point, and I agree with her, was that if they were not going to have full service, they should have been told that when they signed in. Or, as an alternative, their bill should have been reduced. Neither was done.

When she got to our house she was still seething, but having us all agree with her calmed her down a bit. I am surprised she didn't have

Half Way Home

the manager call the home office and get it straightened out, but in true Christmas spirit, she let it drop.

So now we were ready to go to my friends' house for a Christmas supper. As we got ready to go out to the cars, my brother put a hat on his head. Usually he does not wear a hat. In fact, I have never seen him wear a hat in his entire life. But this night he chose to put the most awful, most stupid-looking hat ever on his head.

The hat was not actually so bad in appearance; it just didn't fit his head. It perched on top like a beanie or something. I couldn't believe he didn't know how bad it looked.

"Don't wear the hat," I said.

"Why noth?" answered my brother who was still suffering from the effects of the tooth he broke just as we were beginning our holiday celebration.

"Because it doesn't fit your head and it looks stupid."

"Well, maybe ifth I pulled ith down a lithle bit," he said, grabbing the hat by the edges and pulling it down on his head.

It still looked stupid and it still didn't fit, but I figured it was his hat and his head, so I backed off. Besides his broken tooth would take all the attention away from the hat.

The night went fine at my friends' house. The next morning I took my brother and my parents out to breakfast and sent them on their way. As they left I waved good-bye, feeling as tired as I ever had. And in two hours my in-laws were arriving.

Two weeks later Terry and I finally made our yearly trip to Jekyll Island, Georgia. It was overdue and much needed. It helped us recover from being such good hosts.

In the meantime, my brother got his tooth fixed and now talks the same as he always did. But his hat is missing. Gee, I guess our cat ate it.

Jackie K. Cooper

CHAPTER 3

REFLECTIONS FROM ROUTE 94

Sleep

Sleep is one of my favorite pastimes. It always has been, and I guess always will be. I love to sleep anytime but at night. To go to bed at night always seems to me to be so wasteful. Knowing there are hours and hours in which I could be doing something constructive has always led to my fighting the need to go to bed and sleep.

But, oh how I love to sleep in the afternoon. That is the best possible sleep. To come home early in the afternoon and take a nap is to fall into an untroubled calm and escape from the world. During these periods I go deeper, faster, further into sleep than at any other time.

Someone once told me it was a scientific fact that all sleep before midnight counts as double because it is more restful. I have never been able to find that in the encyclopedia or any medical journal but I like the idea if it is true. It sure does justify my argument for napping.

And if I really want to have a great nap I turn on my trusty fan. The noise of the fan, the feel of the air, the sunlight still around me—they all combine to make this the perfect time to sleep and dream.

When I think back on my childhood some of the happiest moments are those when I was going to sleep. Generally when I recall them I am thinking about it being noon or one in the afternoon at our house. The sun is out in true summer brilliance and a breeze is coming through the open windows of my bedroom.

On the floor beside my bed is my huge airplane propeller fan that my folks gave me when I was about five and that I kept until I got married. As I got older it began to look smaller, but in my remembrances it is strong enough to blow the bedcovers about. And, in my memories, I am lying in front of it, on the bed, and it is lulling me to sleep.

Now did I really enjoy sleeping like I remember? Well, the answer has to be yes. My brother remembers clearly the summer that I spent in a coma-like state. It wasn't a complete coma since I would get up and eat and function for a few hours each day but whenever they missed me they could find me asleep in front of the fan.

It became such a lengthy obsession of mine that my mother finally took me to the doctor to ask for assistance. She explained that I was sleeping all the time. The doctor decided to examine me for some rare illness. He found nothing. When he asked me why I was sleeping all the time I answered him as truthfully as I could. I told him I liked to sleep.

I don't know how much it cost my mother to have the doctor examine me, but the prescription he gave should have been a freebie. He advised she should wake me up when I was sleeping during the day and ban me from the bedroom for any time but nap times and night.

That seemed to work, and after that my sleeping habits became a little bit more normal. That is until I would get upset about something. Then I would immediately become sleepy and nod off. That is something I do to this day. If I am real upset or angry or hurt, watch out. It's into the bedroom I go, and on the bed I lie. Of course, I also turn on my fan just to give the setting the right ambience.

When I wake up I always feel better and more like handling whatever the situation is. Maybe it is a form of sleep therapy or whatever psychiatrists would like to call it. I don't call it anything but escapism, and it works.

So the next time you are really bummed out by the world, escape to your bedroom. Open your windows and let in some fresh air (if it's summer), then turn on an electric fan to drown out the noise of the world and get some air stirring. If things are bothering you enough you will sleep, and when you wake up, I guarantee you will feel better.

If this does work, please make your checks payable to "Sleep Therapist, Jackie K. Cooper" and send them to me.

Half Way Home

Hypochondria—What's Wrong with That?

When you are writing about your life it is always best to be honest, so here goes. It is confession time. I am a little obsessive about my health. Or to put it mildly, I am a raving hypochondriac. My colds tend to border on pneumonia, headaches, or brain tumors. I think it goes back to the fact my mother died of cancer when I was fourteen. From that point on I have been plagued with fears of deadly illnesses.

Luckily I have been blessed with good health for the most part. I have never had a broken bone, and aside from having my tonsils and adenoids out, have never had surgery. One thing I do have, however, are kidney infections. I have had them on and off for twelve years.

A few weeks ago I finally decided to go to a kidney specialist to see if he could find out what caused them. This was my own idea. My regular doctor had not recommended I see a specialist. He said it seemed the infections were just something I was going to have to live with for the time being since they responded to medication and went away after treatment.

But I thought a specialist might know something more. The first thing they did when I got there was a PSA test. I had had the test run before at my regular doctor's, but they did it here again. A PSA is a blood test that is supposed to show up things like cancer symptoms in your body. I am not sure how it works and I am not sure just what it is for, but I know it is an indicator and not an absolute test.

My PSA test came back fine. However, when I told the doctor, whom we will call Dr. Deeds, since he reminded me of Jimmy Stewart in that old movie about a "Mr. Deeds"—or was that Gary Cooper who played him? Anyway, Dr. Deeds was my specialist and I told him about my family history. My mother died of cancer. My father, brother, and first cousin had all had prostate cancer. With this information in mind, Dr. Deeds said maybe we needed to do a biopsy on my prostate.

As soon as he said biopsy, I went into a cold sweat. I suggested maybe we shouldn't do it, but Dr. Deeds was insistent. He said it would give him a chance to see if there was anything wrong that would cause chronic prostatitis, and it would relieve my mind about the possibility of cancer.

The biopsy was scheduled to be done on a Wednesday at the hospital. It would be done on an outpatient basis. I went home and told my wife what the doctor wanted to do. We decided not to tell anyone else, especially my parents. I didn't want to worry them. My father had had prostate cancer seventeen years ago, and my stepmother had had breast cancer shortly after she and my father were married. They didn't need to have another person to worry about in that way.

I did decide to tell my brother. Why, I don't know. I guess I thought his having been through it might ease my mind some. Believe me, it didn't. When I called him and told him he brought forward all my worst fear.

"Yes," he said, "I remember the doctor telling me I needed a biopsy. He didn't see any indication of cancer, but sure enough, when they did the biopsy they found I had it."

I told him about my PSA being low, so I was a little relieved in that sense. It did no good. He assured me he had had a low PSA also. He also described the "needle biopsy" they would do in terms less than encouraging. If anything was going to get me lower than my mood already was, it was this conversation with my brother. I might as well have been talking with Jack "Dr. Death" Kervorkian.

I tried to psych myself up in the most positive of ways as best I could, but I found I was snappier than usual with everyone as I counted off the days to the outpatient surgery. Then my attitude began to be my challenge. I decided no one would be able to say afterwards that I was mean or grumpy waiting to have the test run. I would be "Mr. Nice Guy/Mr. Cheerful" while I waited.

Facing a biopsy is one of the most unpleasant situations possible. Not only do you have the apprehension and dread of wondering what the outcome will be, you also have the fear of the actual pain of the procedure.

I had the prostate biopsy done on a Wednesday. It was done on an outpatient basis and was scheduled the same day that I had an examination of my bladder done. I certainly won't go into specifics, but you had better check all of your modesty at the door when you have these procedures done.

What got me through these tests was the friendliness and professionalism of the people who conducted them. I also have to admit that they were not terribly painful. They caused discomfort but not actual pain.

In the case of the needle biopsy, Dr. Deeds told me it would sting a little. I was prepared for that. What I wasn't prepared for was the sound it made. I swear it sounded like a staple gun being shot. You know the zap sound. When the first shot was fired I almost came up off the table. "Oh, no," said Dr. Deeds, "you can't move." And I didn't. Not after that shock. Again let me stress that it wasn't painful. It was just surprising in its sound, and after the first one I knew what to expect.

That was another surprise. They took six biopsies. From what I was told later this was to insure that a sample from all areas has been taken and examined.

One thing that keeps you calm during all this is the business as usual air of those persons operating the equipment. They don't seem alarmed, so you don't.

Dr. Deeds' nurse stood beside me and patted my foot during the procedure. It was the most tender thing in the world and made me feel comforted in a way that words could never have. It was just one human being having compassion for another and expressing it through a series of pats. I bet she never even knew how much it helped.

Anyway, when all the procedures were over Dr. Deeds said they should have the results on Friday and he would call.

Now began the absolutely worst part of the whole thing—the waiting game. There ought to be some way in this new world of scientific discovery for people not to have to wait two or three days to find out if something is malignant. But that is what happens. You go through the procedure and then you wait and wait and wait.

I found that in those three days of waiting I went through all the classic steps of grieving. At first I was in denial. My mind just refused to think about what might be happening within my body. Then I got angry. I decided it just wasn't fair that this was happening to me at this stage in my life. I had too much I wanted to do. I wanted to grow old enough to retire. I wanted to write the great American novel. I wanted to see my sons married and giving me grandchildren. I still wanted to interview Meryl Streep!

Throughout all these stages I had my faith to cling to. And if you don't have it, you just don't know what a comfort it is. It is truly what gets you through every aspect of something like this.

It took from Wednesday to Friday for me to get the results of the biopsy. And that was three days of sweating bullets. As I said at the start of this story I am a hypochondriac of the worst sort and I just knew when the results came back they were going to be positive.

I called my brother again on the day of the biopsy to tell him all about it. Then I told him I wouldn't get the results until Friday. Since my brother had been through all this himself, I thought maybe this time talking to him would be a comfort. Hah! Not a chance.

"Oh yes," he said, "I remember waiting for the results. The receptionist in the doctor's office called and said the doctor wanted me to come in and see him. I knew when she was the one who called that the test had not come back benign."

Having put that thought in my mind he hung up. Now I knew that if someone other than the doctor called it would be bad news. But on Friday I was told that Diane Keaton was calling. The only Diane Keaton I know is the actress, so I got pretty excited at the thought that she might be actually calling me.

This Diane Keaton was Dr. Deeds' secretary. As soon as I picked up the phone she said in one breath, IworkforDeedsandhewantedmetocallyouandtellyouallyourtestswerenegative." I didn't even have time to panic. She blurted out the good news without even drawing a breath. God bless her!

You can't imagine the weight that was lifted from me unless you have been through this yourself. I felt light as a feather. Since then I have thought back over how I would have reacted had the news not been as good. I have had friends in recent years who did get the news of cancer.

What impresses me is that the people who do have cancer do not see it as a death sentence as well it shouldn't be. There have been so many advances made in the medical field that the recovery rate for all forms of cancer has gotten higher and higher.

The main thing is early detection. This is what I have heard people say over and over and over. And how do you get early detection, well you have yearly checkups and you advise your doctors of any abnormalities you detect in your body. If you are like me you know when something is going on within your body that is not quite right.

When you become aware of something, let the doctor know.

Also, if you are male, have the PSA test run. It is not a sure thing but it is certainly a good indicator of problems with your prostate. And for most men sooner or later you will have problems of this type.

Good health is certainly a blessing. But it is something we too often take for granted until we lose it. Be aware of how blessed you are and live life to the fullest. And when some problems come your way know that you are stronger than you think. And if you aren't, there is a higher presence that is.

Alcohol Can Destroy Your Life

There is a new movie out titled *When a Man Loves a Woman*. I saw it this week. It was romantic, dramatic, and in its final analysis optimistic. It had picture pretty Meg Ryan, and almost as pretty, Andy Garcia, in the leads. She played an alcoholic and he played her bewildered husband.

When you are watching a movie like this, the problems of alcoholism can be fairly upsetting to the audience. But by the time the movie is over the couple on the screen has usually made some progress and there is hope for their lives. That isn't the way it always is in real life, folks.

When I was growing up in South Carolina my best friend from forever was Chuck. I don't remember when he wasn't around. His grandmother lived across the street from us and he was over there a lot, so naturally we became best friends.

I think I knew early on that Chuck didn't have a lot of money, but it wasn't a problem because nobody was rich in my neighborhood. Most of the families were comfortable, but none were on Easy Street. But as I got a little older I learned that everything Chuck had, his grandmother gave to him. Because, you see, both of his parents were alcoholics.

Big Chuck and Minnie, Chuck's parents, were not unkind people. When they were sober they were as nice as any two people could be. The problem was that they were not sober very often. Big Chuck was a genius at repairing cars, so he could make money from time to time. But most of what he made was spent on liquor, so there was very little left over for Chuck.

I think I was the only person Chuck ever let see where he lived. Everybody else was excluded, and rightly so. It was a terrible place—run down, squalid, pathetic. Today it would be condemned and Chuck would be taken away and placed in a foster home. But back then the social conscience of America was not as active. There was no social worker who came out and visited and made sure he was all right. He survived pretty much on his own.

When he got to be twelve or so Chuck got a job in a grocery store bagging groceries. This allowed him to have some money for the necessities, and people in the community pitched in and bought his school books and all. By this time his grandmother had died so he was really on his own as far as family was concerned.

Still Chuck made it through high school and by a stroke of luck found out about some scholarships available and went to college. He was always smart even though his grades didn't show it. But I know if I ever needed any hard subject made easier, all I had to do was talk to Chuck. He understood everything, even the most difficult chemistry problems.

In all the years of knowing Chuck I never heard him say anything bad about his parents. He loved them without exception. They were flawed but he saw that as nature's fault, not theirs. And when they became older he took care of them until they died.

Like I said at the start, not all stories have the happiest of endings. Chuck is now on his fourth marriage and from all reports it is a good one. Still as nice and loving as this new wife is I have fears she won't stick around too long. You see, Chuck has developed a drinking problem. The one man I thought would never take even one drink now takes drink after drink after drink, and he doesn't see anything wrong with it.

I hope Chuck wakes up from this nightmare before it is too late. His health has started failing lately and I blame that on the alcohol. I hope he does too.

Or maybe Chuck will go to see *When a Man Loves a Woman* and see himself in the Meg Ryan role. If the movie serves as a mirror to his life and makes him have some realizations of where he is heading it will have more than served its purpose in being made.

I think I'll send him two tickets.

Time Is Slipping Away

I am on a country music kick again. I just love the way the songs tell stories and reflect life so truly. There is a song I keep hearing that talks about how funny it is that time just slips away, and believe me, whoever wrote those words knows what he/she is talking about. Time just slides by one quick day, one quick year at a time. With my son J. J. getting ready to graduate from college this week, I have never felt those words more.

It seems it was only a couple of years ago when he was born. I can still feel the excitement within my chest as I called my parents to tell them they had a grandson. It was their third grandson but my first son, so the enthusiasm was contagious. I remember my daddy saying how considerate it was of Terry (my wife) to have the baby during his lunch hour. I didn't say it to him, but I think that was the last thing Terry was thinking about at that time.

In no time at all J. J. was in kindergarten, grammar school, and then high school. It was in high school when he was thirteen years old that he began his writing career. He and his friend, Michael Potts began to cover the Westfield football games for *The Houston Home Journal* of Perry.

He continued to do this for all of his high school years but it was pretty difficult when he first started since he couldn't drive. Either the Potts family or Terry and I had to transport J. J. and Michael to the games and then make sure they got the story to the paper after it was written.

Michael's interests eventually went elsewhere but J. J. stuck with writing. He had always loved sports, so writing about them was a natural extension of this passion. And he proved to be good at it. Now you may think that is just a father's natural pride coming through but the state of Georgia must have felt the same way since he was one of the youngest persons ever to receive an award from the Georgia Press Association for sports writing.

It always amazed me that he could love sports so much. I thought maybe my love of movies would rub off on him but he always preferred to watch the Super Bowl or the World Series. Sometimes I watched it with him, and "sometimes" (rarely) he watched the Oscar show with me.

It also amazed me how J. J. could keep a bunch of statistics in his head or on a sheet of paper and then transcribe them into a readable, enjoyable article. I do think that maybe he got the ability to provide a personal interest aspect to his stories from me. I know he didn't gain the sports acumen from my genes.

Anyway, this Friday my family will be traveling up to Athens for the ceremonies at the School of Journalism. Grandparents from both sides of the family will join us there, as will some of our friends. We will celebrate J. J.'s achievements and his college career.

Terry and I were prepared for J. J. to end up taking a job anywhere in the country. We hoped he would be offered something close to home but we didn't have our hopes up too high. So you can imagine our joy when he found the best job and it was Macon, Georgia.

When you read the Macon paper and see his stories you will know what an excellent writer he is. And if you are fortunate enough to get to know him personally, you will discover what an excellent person he is. He bears my name and my pride. He is my first-born, my J. J.

Another Graduation Day

Well, we made it through J. J.'s graduation. Did we have a good time? Yes. Were there any potholes in the road to graduation day? Yes, Yes, Yes.

Any time you try to assemble a group of family and friends for a celebration there is bound to be a little confusion and trouble. Especially when people are coming from different cities and states. When J. J. graduated the grandparents came from Florida and South Carolina. And we, along with son Sean, Sean's girlfriend Paula, and other friends made the trip from Perry.

At first it was planned that Terry's parents and my parents would assemble in Perry on Thursday night and then we would all drive to Athens on Friday. But then I discovered that it was closer to Athens from Clinton, South Carolina, than it was from Clinton to Perry.

I called my folks and offered that they might want to just meet us in Athens for the graduation ceremonies and then come on home to Perry after that. They agreed. I then called J. J. in Athens and had him tell me a good meeting place on the road from Clinton for me to meet up with the folks.

J. J. isn't the best at giving directions, and my stepmother isn't the best at receiving them, and it is especially confusing when I am the in-between man relaying information back and forth. Still we made plans to meet at the First American Bank in Athens at 3:00 P.M. Friday.

Terry's parents got into Perry from St. Pete at 6:00 P.M. Thursday. We hadn't been expecting them until around midnight, but they had left earlier than expected. I hate surprises. When somebody tells me they will be at my house at midnight, I don't expect them until midnight. If they had to ride around for six hours, they could have done that and still gotten to my house at midnight like they said they would. That's one of my quirks, but it is a big one.

On Friday we left Perry around noon in order to get to Athens at the rendezvous time. We took our time and when we got to the outskirts of Athens I called J. J. to see if he had heard from the grandparents. He said they had called a few minutes earlier and were waiting at the bank.

When we got to where they were waiting, Daddy announced that he had driven the whole way and that it had only taken them two and a half hours. Two and a half hours! It's only 104 miles. I figure they averaged about forty miles an hour down the road. Wouldn't you have loved to have been behind them?

My Daddy will be eighty years old this year, so you can imagine my fears when he gets behind the wheel. But the state of South Carolina keeps issuing him a driver's license and he keeps moving on down the road. You may find this hard to believe but he sees better now than he did ten years ago. The doctors say he has gotten his second sight. Have you ever heard of that happening?

So his second sight and his high threshold of pain keep him in pretty good shape. My stepmother was already tiring when they got out of the car in Athens, but Daddy was smiling and saying how good he felt.

Anyway, I know it did J. J.'s heart good to look out and see a whole row of family and friends cheering him on as he got his diploma. I was about to burst with pride and it got even greater when they announced he was graduating "cum laude."

He looks like his mother. He got his brains from his mother. He is a wonderful person, just like his mother. Me, I am just the busting-with-pride father.

The Great Flood of 1994

Mark my words, it will go down in the history books as the Great Flood of 1994—at least in my history book. Last summer I sat and watched the Midwest floods, feeling so sorry for those people out there and thankful that I lived in Georgia where that could never happen. Hello! Wake up call! It did.

All through the days of the deluge I kept thinking it couldn't be happening. I guess it hit home one day when I was trying to get to my home in Perry from Warner Robins. I drove down 247 to Bonaire and then took 96 over to I-75. It was all smooth driving until I got to 75 and there I found the interstate had been closed going south.

I couldn't believe it. It was like one of those cheesy horror films where the streets are deserted. The interstate stretched out like a big vacant nothing. I quickly passed over the bridge and headed for other roads that might take me to Perry but none were to be found.

Finally realizing I wasn't going to drive to Perry anytime soon, I decided to park my car and walk home. Yes walk. Me, who can't do any form of physical exercise without culture shock was going to hoof it "x" number of miles home.

I drove into the driveway at the sod farm near the Interstate since I know Linda and Larry Johnson who work there, so I knew my car would be safe there. As I was parking I saw some friends of mine, Rick and Martha Davis, who also planned to hike to Perry. Suddenly I was part of a caravan.

Now Rick and Martha had things under control. First off, they had keys to the office at the sod farm, so we were able to make a rest stop before we started our trek. Secondly, they had Cokes to take along with us. And thirdly, they had a portable phone. If we weren't yuppie walkers, nobody was.

Just as we started out another friend, Jimmy Harrell, drove up. He had a truck and said we might be able to go down to 247 and take it out to the brewery and get in the back way. Sounded good to the three of us so we piled in and started out.

We got all the way out to the brewery turn off and got turned back. So the walk began to loom large in our thoughts again. Like Melanie, Scarlett, and Mammy we were going to get home to Tara. No Yankees (or floods) were going to keep us from going home.

But once again as we formulated our walk plans, something else changed. The highway patrol was now letting people going south drive down one lane of the northbound interstate. So that's what we did and finally got to Perry.

Now that was only a mild inconvenience. I have heard horror stories from other people who were stuck away from home for days. I guess they didn't want to walk like I was prepared to do.

I marvel too at the kindness of people in bad situations. In the middle of all the flood trouble I was trying to get a plaque made for my father's eightieth birthday. I went to the shop where I was supposed to pick it up but the shop was closed.

A lady sitting outside in one of those big recreational vehicles told me no one was there. I noticed the RV was plugged into the electrical outlet on the front of the building.

When I got home I called the emergency number of the shop. I asked the lady who owned it if she knew a big RV was sucking power out of her building.

"Oh yes," she answered, "they called me and asked if it was all right. They were stuck trying to go south. They said they would put some money under the door but I told them to use what they wanted and forget it."

I was amazed at her charity, but heart-warmed that someone would be that kind to strangers. I guess as long as we have people like her the world will be an okay place—and we will all be able to survive tragedies like the Great Flood of 1994.

Going Home

It is hard for me to believe that when I went back to my hometown of Clinton, South Carolina, recently it was the first time I had been there in a couple of years. Most of the time my parents come to see me rather than vice versa. But this was the occasion of my father's eightieth birthday and my stepmother was planning a celebration so it was necessary for me to make the trip.

My sons went up for the day while Terry and I spent the night and came back the next day. We couldn't stay long because my father's birthday was on Saturday and my son J. J.'s was the next day. So we had to rush home to celebrate his day too.

At the gathering to celebrate my father's birthday a lot of his friends were present. They are all about his age and it amazes me how good they look. Now my father has had some health problems and is a little frail but the rest of these people look fantastic!

My stepmother's sister turned eighty the Monday after Daddy turned eighty on Saturday and she doesn't look a day over sixty. I mean not a day! I asked her the secret to her health and she just said eighty wasn't what it used to be. And isn't that the truth.

It seems to me that back when I was growing up when a person reached sixty they had one foot in the grave and looked it. I mean they were all either bald or silver-haired. They had hearing aids and thick glasses. Their skin sagged and their stomachs pooched. Nowadays septuagenarians and octogenarians have streamlined physiques and healthy looking skin. And this isn't even talking about the ones who have had plastic surgery.

Now isn't it a pleasant thought that you can look good and feel good for years to come. I know it gives me hope. Of course, if I exercised more and watched what I ate more, I would have better health. But it is so hard to do. And now they are saying everything I like is bad for me. It was bad enough when they said popcorn was bad for your cholesterol. Now they have added Mexican food to the list.

Pretty soon there isn't going to be anything you can eat and feel confident that you are being health conscious.

Anyway, while I was home I walked around the old neighborhood. Now it does look eighty years old. The houses have shrunk and they all could use a new coat of paint. I looked at the house where I grew up. It is right next door to the house where my father and stepmother live today. The house looks like a dollhouse it is so small. But somehow it held two adults and two children for a lot of years.

There is a fenced-in backyard where my brother and I used to play and I can remember having races from one end of the yard to the other. It seemed like we ran for miles. Now it looks like it is maybe three or four good strides.

Then there is the back porch. The first time I tried to jump off of it I felt like I was on top of the Empire State Building. There was no way I could fall from that distance and not be killed. I don't know how long it took before I got up my nerve but eventually I did jump. But why? What makes kids want to jump from things? I remember the kids in my neighborhood were always jumping from anything that was off the ground.

All those kids are gone from the neighborhood now. Most have moved out of Clinton but a few have remained. The few I did run into looked a lot older than me—at least I thought they did. They looked good—but older than me.

It does you good to go back to your hometown every now and then. It stirs up a lot of memories and emotions but it makes you feel good too. I had a childhood like kids today don't have. I played in a neighborhood where I felt totally safe from sunup to sundown. I rode my bike to the movies and my parents rarely worried. It was another world, or so it seems.

Jackie K. Cooper

The Giant of Las Vegas

There are giants living in our country as I found out recently when I visited Las Vegas. Big, big giants who are out there waiting for the unwary visitor. Now I didn't know these giants were out there until I arrived, but I had heard of them and had some idea of who and what they were.

The reason I made the trip to Las Vegas was to attend the Video Software Dealers Association (VSDA) convention. I had gotten press credentials for the gathering and thought it would be a fun week. I mean who couldn't have fun in Las Vegas.

Plus my friend Randy from California was coming as well as his friend Mitch from Louisiana. That would make three of us sharing a room so the expenses would not be great. I got a ticket out and back through my frequent flyer miles, so the entire trip was nominal in cost.

Terry and I had driven through Las Vegas on our way back to Georgia from California, when we finished our two-year time of living out there. But that was twelve years ago and I had not been back since.

When I got off the plane in Las Vegas the first thing I noticed was there are slot machines in the airport. They are everywhere and there are loads of people playing them. I wondered to myself if these were people catching flights, tourists, or people who just came to the airport to play slot machines. Who knows!

I checked in and stayed in the room long enough to hang up a few clothes and then headed down to the casino. Once there I staked out a "Video Poker" machine (5-cent variety) and prepared for a long night.

Now I am not a big gambler. I enjoy the fun of playing even though I don't expect to make the "big" payoff. I like to sit and put in my nickels and talk to the people who sit down beside me.

My machine (I always have a favorite machine) was located next to a hall that led down to the elevators that ran up to the rooms.

Although there was a place for children to play games on the floor below the casino, people would bring their children to the hallway and tell them to stay there while they went and gambled.

The kids, of course, didn't like this. They would either stay there a while and then wander into the casino, or they would start to cry and holler. I saw people bring babies in baby strollers and leave them there. And that made me furious. But the Greed Giant loved it and fed upon it.

One little boy kept coming over to my machine and talking to me. He asked where I was from, what I was doing, and how long I was staying—just kid talk. The attendant came over and told me I could not have a child at the machine.

I explained he wasn't my child. She asked where his parents were and he said his Dad was playing cards. She told him he would have to stand in the hallway away from the machines. As soon as she left he was back. And in a few seconds she was back. Once again she told me he could not be at the machines, and once again I told her he was not my son.

Now the lady attendant was angry and she took the boy to find his father. A few minutes later the father and son passed by my machine with the father screaming at his son for not staying where he was supposed to be.

Greed is the giant in Las Vegas—a very big giant.

No Evil Stepmothers Here

Once upon a time there was a boy of fourteen who adored his mother. They were as close as a mother and son could be. He loved his father and brother but there was nobody like his mother. There was a special bond between them.

But as happens in life sometimes, the boy's mother died. It was virtually the end of his world. Everything that had been good was now bad, and everything bad was now worse. It was the darkest of times.

The boy's father had one son in college and one son almost paralyzed by despair. He felt helpless. He turned to a friend of the family, a woman he had known for years. And out of his need he found love.

The man and woman married and the young boy was even more devastated. Here was a new person trying to come in and take his mother's place. It was unacceptable, and he went about showing her how unacceptable it was.

Over the years the war of words and actions ebbed and flowed. Some days were worse than others, some were almost passable. As the young man got older it seemed the gulf between him and his stepmother could never be bridged.

It did improve, however, when the young man got married. His new bride liked this stepmother from the start, but the young man still harbored resentment and distrust. Things rocked on until his children were born. This is when his stepmother blossomed. She knew she could never be the young man's mother for he had too many memories, but she could be these boys' grandmother with no competition from the past.

Over the years the man and his stepmother arrived at a truce of sorts. But it still wasn't what it should be. Even though he prayed for a solution, he knew it would take a miracle.

The miracle arrived with the failure of his father's health. As the older man got more and more infirm, the wife became more and more caring for him. And the young man began to see their love more

Half Way Home

clearly and how it was a miracle in and of itself. The stepmother did everything for his father and more. If she could have breathed for him she would have done that too and gladly.

The older man is still alive and doing fairly well. The young man sees them as often as he can but even when he is not with them he doesn't worry. His stepmother has everything under control or as much as it can be with an eighty-year-old man who is not in great health.

Now when the young man talks with his father he always asks to talk to his stepmother too. They talk about everything and they are completely relaxed as they do it. And when it is time to hang up the phone he tells each of them how much he loves them, and he means it.

Stepmothers have gotten a bad reputation over the years. From reading all those old fairy tales you know they are destined to be considered the enemy. But I am living proof it doesn't always have to be that way. This is my story and it is full of love and miracles. And we are all living happily ever after.

Sundays of the Past

Sunday was a big day for our family when I was growing up. For one thing, it was the only day my Daddy didn't work. He worked the six other days from sunup to sundown but Sunday was his day of rest.

We always went to church as a family. In my memory it seems all those Sundays were bright and sunny. I can remember being able to stretch out on the pew between my mother and father and as the preacher presented his sermon I drifted off to sleep. I guess in a way that is a backhanded compliment to the church.

We were a Southern Baptist family and members of the First Baptist Church of Clinton, South Carolina. The only preacher I knew from the time I was born until I graduated from high school was Brother Darr. His first name was Joseph, but everyone in the church called him Brother Darr.

He was a very formal man. So formal that I don't think I ever saw him dressed in less than a suit and tie. Legend had it he even mowed his lawn in a suit and tie. I never witnessed that event but it is what all of us kids told one another and always related to any newcomer.

Brother Darr was a fire and brimstone preacher and could get red in the face as he preached against the evils of sin! But he was also one of the nicest people I have ever met. So even when he was turning red in the face I still felt comforted by his sermons. So comforted I could drift off to sleep.

After church we usually had dinner at home. We were not wealthy people in any sense of the word though every now and then we did go out to "Louie's Restaurant." There I would always order a hot roast pork sandwich—the kind that was open faced with gravy all over everything. I can still remember how delicious it was to this very day.

Most times, though, we ate at home. My mother was a good cook, although not a particularly adventurous one. I can remember us having country-style steak, fried chicken, or spaghetti on most of these Sundays. And if it was a special day we would have either banana pudding (my brother's favorite) or strawberry shortcake (my favorite) for dessert.

My Daddy worked for the Merita Bread Company so we always had bread products on hand. Merita made a special shortcake dessert shell. Mother would ladle the strawberries over this and then she would spray on whipped cream. Was it good? You betcha!

In my memory bank are etched the glow of those Sundays gone by. They are special memories and ones that will be with me always. So you can understand why a sign I saw on the way to Jekyll Island a few weeks ago meant so much to me. My wife, Terry, and I were driving through the list of small towns that dot the road on the way to that seacoast resort.

As we passed through the heart of one, I looked over and saw a sign on a Dairy Queen. In bold letters it stated, "Jesus Loves You—and Strawberry Shortcake." For this son of the South, that said it all.

Left in the Woods

Just about everyone who knows me knows I am a fan of country music. But not everyone knows I am also a big fan of Broadway composers. Now I know these two kinds of entertainment are worlds apart but I have an appreciation of both. Broadway show tunes are as close to opera and classical music as I will ever come.

One of my favorite Broadway composers is Stephen Sondheim and one of his best shows, in my opinion, is *Into the Woods*. I have the music on CD and play it over, and over, and over. Just ask my wife, who is probably ready to toss the CD in the nearest trash bin.

In this play one of the songs has words that describe people leaving you when you are only halfway through the woods. Now that isn't on first listening a very poignant line, but for me it causes my heart to ache and break. For the longest time I didn't know why, but recently I discovered the answer to the pain it invokes

A good friend of mine lost her mother a few weeks ago. Seeing her go through that loss brought back the loss occasioned by my own mother's death. Well, it didn't so much bring it back as it just made it fresher. I don't think there is a day, or certainly not a week, that passes that I don't think of her in some way.

I think of how she never got to see me graduate from high school, college, or law school; how she never met my wife or saw my sons; how she will never see her grandchildren; how she never saw how I looked as a man.

My mother was special, but then I think that all mothers are special. But some are more special than others and mine was very special to me. In the fourteen years we knew each other a bond was formed that has lasted a lifetime.

My friend's mother was older than mine was when she died and my friend had her in her life for many more years than mine was in mine. But, So what? I don't care if you lose someone at twenty, thirty, forty, or more; it still hurts just the same. Pain is pain and length of time a loved one has lived is no consolation.

Going through life is like walking through the woods. We never know what dangers are lurking there or what happiness is around any corner. To get us through this trip it is nice to be surrounded by people we love. And as we go through the woods we meet more and more people who share our journey and our life.

Still no matter how many people we meet, the loss of any person is tragic. When my mother died, a piece of my heart stopped functioning. And as others have gone away the same has occurred.

My mother left me when I was just entering the forest of life. It wasn't her choice to leave. I am sure she would have liked to have stayed with me for a long, long part of my journey. But that wasn't to be.

I will never get over the loss. I have, and I will experience joy, happiness, excitement, and anticipation, but in a way I will always be diminished.

Name That Child

How important is the name a child is given? Does the name give any special prestige, or does it detract from who the child becomes? Isn't it true that a rose by any other name would still smell as sweet?

Recently a friend of mine was telling me how horrified he was that his son and daughter-in-law had named their new daughter July. To him, naming the child after the month of her conception was a stupid and idiotic thing to do. He insists that he is going to call her Ann, which is her middle name.

Now you can imagine this poor young girl's identity problems when she starts responding to everyone calling her July except for her grandfather who insists on calling her Ann. Here's hoping my friend relents before he causes too much family friction and harm to the child.

Names can be problems. When we had our first son my wife was determined he should be a junior. I, who had had enough problems with the name Jackie Cooper, was not as eager to pass the name along. So we settled on a compromise. He would be named Jackie Kershaw Cooper Jr., but he would be called "J. J." (as in Jackie Junior).

Just about everyone accepted these two letters to be his name, except for his maternal grandmother. She kept asking us when we were going to give him a real name. We would always answer that we had, and it was J. J.

Now it is impossible for me to think of him in any other way. Sometimes I get his mail and I always open it, thinking it is for me. I never think of him as Jackie. And I am pleased his by-line in the sports section of the newspaper is always J. J. Cooper.

You would think that maybe by the time we had our second son we would have learned our lesson and would have given him a run-of-the-mill name. But no! We both decided on "Sean" almost immediately. He was born on St. Patrick's Day, so Sean Christopher Cooper seemed to be the appropriate name for him.

Half Way Home

I will never forget a friend of mine asking me where we got the name "See Ann." That's the way it looked to him and that is the way he pronounced it. We have also had people pronounce it "Seen" or "Shawn." It is neither. It is Sean, pronounced "Shahn." This is the same way Sean Connery pronounces his name.

My brother's family hasn't produced run-of-the-mill names either. When he and I were growing up he went by "Tommy." When he went to college the first letter he wrote back to us was signed "Thomas." Then after he got married he began to be known as "Thom." That to me was pretty pretentious. And it just made me that much more determined to remain "Jackie."

My brother's oldest son was named for him. His name is Thomas Bobo Cooper, Jr. Bobo was my paternal grandmother's maiden name. So Thom's son was called "Bo." You can imagine the kidding he got with that handle. He was "Bobo the Clown" or "B. O." Bo, a musician, is now touring with Christian singer Steven Curtis Chapman. He is billed as "Boh." Go figure.

My name has caused me problems for two reasons. First, many people just don't like for a man to be named Jackie. It just pains them to have to say it. I can't begin to tell you how many times I have met someone and introduced myself as Jackie Cooper and then had them turn around and call me Jack.

Jack is not my name. My name is Jackie. On my birth certificate it is listed as "Jackie Kershaw Cooper." So Jackie is not my nickname.

Secondly, there is the identification with Jackie Cooper, the actor. From day one I have been asked if I was named for him. The answer is no! I was named for my Uncle Aubrey. Confused? I bet you are. Well, it's simple. My Uncle Aubrey was nicknamed "Jack," and my mother named me after him. It makes sense in a slightly warped way.

When I was growing up most of my friends called me Cooper. I liked that. But I couldn't be known as Cooper Cooper. In law school I went by the name "Chip." Don't ask me why, I couldn't tell you.

I am satisfied with being called Jackie. I think it suits me. My wife likes it, and that is good enough for me.

Insurance for the Mind

Do you ever think about what makes a town a good place to live? I do. I have a few requisites for a place to fit into this category. They are: an active church community, friendly neighbors, a strong police force, and a good public library. Many of you might have guessed the first three but might have not listed the fourth.

I am a firm believer in good libraries and have been all my life. When I was growing up in Clinton, South Carolina, the public library and the college library were the same thing. Since I have always loved to read, I made my way there as soon as I knew it existed.

Mrs. Gray was the children's librarian. Her hair was as gray as her name, and her warmth would put the sun to shame. Every Saturday morning was a wonderful time when she would gather with her "special friends" and read to them. I can't begin to tell you how magical that time with her was, and through her voice and wonderful stories I traveled the universe and had adventure upon adventure.

Some of my best friends resided in Mrs. Gray's books. Once I met the Bobbsey Twins and the Hardy Boys, I had friends who would stay with me for a lifetime. And in my imagination they were as real to me as the kids who lived down the street.

Later on I lived in places like Columbia, South Carolina; Rocky Mount, North Carolina; and Warner Robins, Georgia. At each stop I made sure I checked out the library so that my family and I could have access to the books and magazines we love.

When we first thought about moving to Perry, Georgia, I went to see what kind of library was located here. At that time Alice Gilbert was the head librarian, and as soon as I met her I knew my family would be all right when it came to books. Alice loves to read as much, or more, than I do, and anyone who has that interest knows how important a good library is.

Over the years I have used the library to the fullest. And so have my wife and sons. The boys used it for research for school projects

Half Way Home

and Terry used it for teaching information. Our library cards are as essential to us as our drivers' licenses.

It is so great to read or hear about a bestseller and then be able to pick up the phone and tell whoever answers to "put it on reserve." Then in just a short while there is a message on my answering machine saying the book is there. Of course, it takes someone with my speed reading skills to be able to finish a voluminous Tom Clancy novel in one week. But I can understand the reason to limit the time of lending, so another person can then enjoy the book.

With this background of library enjoyment you can imagine my shock when I heard the other day that the local system may be in jeopardy. From what I have learned the funding for the library is going to be cut and in having this happen, the library as we know and love it may cease to exist.

Now I am not a very political animal, so I don't know how or why or who and what is causing this to happen. But for whatever reasons someone thinks that a city or county like ours can exist without a library, they are wrong. We need the facility to stay just as it is, with no tampering. This is for the sake of all adults who live in our area and especially for our children.

For anyone who thinks a library is just an unnecessary luxury, think again. A library is health insurance for the mind. If we ever lose it, we will long regret it. So whatever it takes to preserve the system we have, let's do it!

Jackie K. Cooper

Santa Claus, Georgia

It is hard for me to believe the holiday season is back so quickly. It must be old age, but time is flying by, and the seasons are coming rapidly on the heels of the preceding ones. In anticipation of Christmas, the movie theaters have already started showing Christmas products. One of these is the Tim Allen film *The Santa Clause.*

I went to California a few weeks ago for an advance showing of the movie and a chance to talk with Mr. Allen. Little did I know that in just a few weeks the movie would be making a special appearance in, of all places, Vidalia, Georgia. But that is what happened last week. The Brice Theater in that town was host for a one-night preview showing of the film.

The reason for the screening was the little community of Santa Claus, Georgia. This town, which is located south of Lyons, was selected by the Walt Disney Studios to have a special showing based on its name. Dave Tribble of the Michael Parver Agency in Atlanta, which represents Disney in our area, got the idea of having the showing and brought it to fruition.

Now the town of Santa Claus has about 250 people who live there, and just about all of them were in the Brice Theater on the night of the showing. Mayor Bernard Harden said the town had been very excited about being selected and showed their enthusiasm by their participation.

Mayor Harden gave me some background on Santa Claus, Georgia. He said the town was formed in 1941 and grew up around a roadside stand in a pecan orchard. The man who owned the stand gave the city its name. At first it was named Santa Clause, just like the movie, but a few years ago the town fathers discovered the misspelling and had to petition the legislature to have the "e" dropped.

All of the streets in the town have Christmas associations. For example, the city hall is located at 25 December Drive. Each year many, many people send their cards to the city to have them postmarked "Santa Claus, Georgia." Mayor Harden said they got more than 12,000 pieces of mail last year and expect even more this year.

The reason the movie was screened in Vidalia instead of Santa Claus was because there is no movie theater in Santa Claus. The Brice Theater in Vidalia is one of those big screen theaters, which hardly exist any more. Most have been cut down to bi-screen or tri-screen size.

The owner-operator of the Brice Theatre is Barron Godby and he is one of the last independent theater owners. He was proudly beaming at all the excitement the screening of the film was causing. And the audience responded to the film with the appropriate cheers and tears.

When I interviewed Tim Allen in California he said: "I wanted to make sure the movie didn't focus on the commercial aspect of the season, but rather stressed the spiritual side. This is such an important part of the Christian belief that I didn't want to take away from it in any way." The people who watched *The Santa Clause* in Vidalia seemed to get the message he was sending and stayed in the spirit of the season with their responses.

One man told me this was the most exciting thing that had ever happened in Santa Claus—even if it did happen in Vidalia, too. On this very special night the beard of St. Nicholas and the ears of Mickey Mouse joined together to bring Hollywood to Georgia, and to spread a little movie magic around the community.

That Old Gang of Mine

A few weeks ago I made the trip back to Clinton, South Carolina, for my thirty-fifth high school reunion. It was a trip back in time I didn't especially want to make. Well, that is not entirely true. When we had our twentieth reunion, it was great. But add another fifteen years onto the time gap and you have a possibly boring evening.

At least I knew I would get to see my two best friends Chuck and Hollis, and I did. They came to my parents' house as soon as Terry and I arrived. Hollis had a heart attack a few years ago and it aged him a lot. Even though he is now doing fine, he looks like Father Time—gray hair and graybeard.

Chuck, on the other hand looks relatively young (like me!) But he is so intense these days that he drives me crazy. Everything to him is something to be analyzed. He can't just say he liked a movie, he has to tell you why—in detail! And God forbid that you should talk politics with him. There is no view but his view.

Still it was good to have them around and learn what was happening in their lives. Hollis is still teaching school, but plans to retire this year. Chuck is a research chemist and loves his work.

Our reunion consisted of a banquet and then a program. Three of the women in our graduating class had taken it upon themselves to organize the event, and they did an excellent job. The tables were decorated nicely and the pictures and banners on the wall were fine.

The first person I spied when we walked in was a real quiet girl from our class. I walked over and said hello and asked how she had been doing. "I was fine until my husband dropped dead two months ago," she responded. That set the tone of the evening.

It seemed everybody I talked to had either just lost a spouse or a parent. Or they had a parent who was in a home and not liking it. Happy conversation was not the order of the day.

Then there was the fact that I barely remembered anybody. I am not very good with names under the best of circumstances and with this large group saying hello, I was at loss. Now they did have on

122   Half Way Home

nametags, but with my trifocal eyes I either had to stare at the stupid card or wing it. Mostly I tried to wing it.

As the evening drew to an end, people were telling each other good-bye and adding we would have to get together again. As they said this to me, inside my mind I was saying to myself, "Why?" Why would we get together and what would we talk about if we did? There has been too much water over the dam to recapture long lost friendships and relationships.

Will I go back if we have a fortieth reunion? Probably so. Like the moth drawn to the flame most of us have a compelling need to see if our contemporaries have survived as well as we. It gives us a last shred of immortality to hold on to.

By the way, my friend Hollis loved it all. He was voted "Most Changed." He thought it was a compliment. Are we living on the same planet?

Another Christmas Story

Whenever I hear the song "Have Yourself a Merry Little Christmas" I think about how hard it is at times to honor that simple wish. For thousands and possibly more people across the country the Christmas season is a time for sadness and depression. The brighter the light, the dimmer the happiness in the hearts of some.

The other day somebody told me they would be so glad when Christmas was over and they could get on with their life. All the problems with getting the right Christmas present were more of a hassle than they could handle. It would be easier to face the dreariness of January than to cope with the cheeriness of December.

Maybe some of our problems relate to the fact we glorify Christmases past. In memory, the holidays of our childhood always had a rosier glow than those of more recent vintage. But in reality, everything about those long ago Christmases was not really perfection.

A friend of mine was telling me a few days ago about the Christmases of his youth. He added that his grandmother's cooking for the Christmas holidays was legendary. She would cook and cook and cook. There was food everywhere. More than he and his family could ever eat—or would want to! It seems what everyone forgets in reliving those memories was the fact that his grandmother was a lousy cook. She was famous more for volume than for quality.

Another friend of mine said she and her sister always got into major fights at Christmas. It seems that whatever her sister got was what she had really wanted, and vice versa. The siblings would end up getting into actual physical fights and roll around the living room floor beating on each other. Their parents always threatened that the next Christmas Santa Claus wasn't going to bring them anything. But in the intervening year's time, these threats were forgotten.

At my house it was always me and my disappointments. I always wanted a "surprise" for Christmas. I didn't know what it was, but I knew that if I actually got it I would recognize that this was the surprise I had been awaiting. Sound complicated? It was. And the sad thing was that my poor mother worried herself crazy over what this "longed for surprise" could be.

Every Christmas morning my brother would wake me up. I always wanted to sleep on until later, but he would insist I get up at the crack of dawn. So into the living room we would hurry. There he would ooh and ah over each and every gift he had gotten. I, on the other hand, would give a cursory glance and announce that I hadn't gotten my surprise. Then I would go back to bed. What a rotten attitude! What a rotten kid!

Yes, those misty-eyed remembrances of glorious Christmases past just don't really tell the true picture. The ones we are having today may even be brighter and better.

So what can we do for the people who say, "Just get me through Christmas"? Well, we can be supportive and understanding, for it is true that Christmas is hard for some. We can also help people move the emphasis from what is Christmas doing for—or to—me to what can I do for someone else.

To my way of thinking, the best Christmases ever are those where we think of others ahead of ourselves. When you are full of thoughts of doing for others, you almost forget all the problems involving what is happening to you.

The secret of the season is to be merry and reflective and joyous and thankful, as best we can. And for many, many of us, it is a time to be grateful for the true meaning of the season which is the anniversary of the birth of Jesus Christ.

Jackie K. Cooper

CHAPTER 4

REFLECTIONS FROM ROUTE 95

Growing Old

One of my wife's favorite sayings is that when she gets to Heaven she is going to have a list of questions ready for God. Well, when I get there I am going to have a list too, and at the top of my list is going to be an inquiry as to the rationale for growing old. Now I know there are some rare instances where the golden years are some of the best, but for the most part it seems to me that getting on in age is no reward but the booby prize.

I think it was Art Linkletter who said, "Growing old isn't for sissies." He had his most perceptive hat on the day he made that observation. Growing old isn't a picnic. At least I don't think my father is having any great time.

He and my stepmother spent a few days with me and my family at Christmastime. It made for my most depressing Christmas ever. Every time I looked at him my heart wanted to break. I know the virile, happy, healthy father I once knew was in there somewhere but I rarely glimpsed him.

To begin with, my father has lost more than fifty pounds. The doctors say he is physically in pretty good shape but he just won't eat. Now this is a man who taught me that you should never waste food. It used to be when he sat down to a meal he met each serving with gusto. Now he just picks at what is there and eats little.

There is also the matter of his pills and his eye drops. He takes pills for high blood pressure, diabetes, cholesterol control, and a million other things. He puts drops in his eyes to maintain the right balance of liquids there. After each meal my stepmother counts out his pills and sets out his eye drops. He takes the pills without objection and uses the eye drops religiously.

But, a few minutes after he has done all this the questioning starts. "Did I take my pills, Florence?" he asks. She assures him he did. A few more minutes and he says, "Don't I need to take my pills, Florence?" She again assures him he has. This goes on and on and on until you want to scream your head off. But each time she answers him patiently that he is all right.

I told her that I don't know what would happen to Daddy if something happened to her. I would try to care for him, but I couldn't do it like she does. She said the reason is that Daddy is her life and I have a life of my own. I guess that is true.

Thankfully there is still some humor in their lives. One day at the table after Daddy had asked about his pills 900 times he turned to Florence and told her he was sorry to be so much trouble, "You aren't too much trouble, Tom," she assured him. "If you were I would have pushed you out of the car on the way down here. I would have told Jackie we hit a little bump and out the door you went." Daddy got a good chuckle out of that.

I know I am not the only person alive with elderly parents. It seems to be something I see more and more every day. And when I talk to people who share my feelings and my concerns it helps some. But I still feel guilty. Guilty about not doing more, not saying more, not being there.

God must have a reason for creating old age. I just wish I knew what it is.

And Not a Crumb to Eat

This Christmas past was one of the most depressing I have ever spent due to my father's declining health. It was also one for the books as far as bizarre occurrences too.

On Christmas Day we got up, had breakfast, went to church, came home, had a light lunch, and then opened our gifts. We ate lightly because we were going to a friend's home for a Christmas evening meal. But as we were opening our gifts, the phone rang. It was our friends saying they were sick and would have to cancel the evening get-together. No problem, we thought, we'll just go out to eat. Boy, were we naive!

I checked around that afternoon and discovered one of the steak houses was open in Macon. So, later that afternoon, we drove up to J. J.'s apartment in Macon so my parents could see it. I also had J. J. call ahead and make reservations for seven people at the steakhouse. We made them for 7:00 P.M.

Our son Sean and his girlfriend, Paula, were in one car; J. J. was in his, while Terry, Daddy, Florence, and I were in mine. We don't crowd up when we travel anywhere. We just form a caravan and get going. Anyway, we proceeded to the steakhouse at 7:00 P.M. on the nose.

The hostesses at this place were straight out of the "valley girl dictionary." When I told the hostess we were the Coopers and had a reservation for seven at seven, she replied, "Cool!" You notice she didn't say, "Right this way." That didn't happen for fifteen more minutes, while we cooled our heels waiting.

When we finally made it to our table the waiter appeared and took our drink orders. He was back with them in a flash. Then he took out his pad to take our dinner orders. I decided to go first and ordered a rib-eye steak.

"We're all out of rib-eyes," he replied. "We also are out of chicken and sirloins."

What he had left were the most expensive items on the menu. A consensus was quickly taken and we decided to leave. By this time it was close to eight o'clock and my group was getting hungry. Now, why the steakhouse didn't tell us what they were out of while we were waiting, I don't know. I guess it was just a night for surprises.

So off we went to restaurant number two. This one was a general food place and all of its lights were on. It was like a refuge in the storm of hunger for my group. But there was a line. A long line of people waiting to get in, get seated, and fed.

We did find a place for Daddy and Florence to sit while we waited. The rest of us stood in the line. I had J. J. growling in my ear that this was ridiculous and that he was going to go back to his place and eat warmed-over spaghetti. In the other ear Sean was saying how stupid it was that we didn't have food at our house. Terry was standing in line with a glazed look on her face.

When we finally got seated the waitress came over to take our order. She was not happy to see us. She was not happy to be working on Christmas night. She was not happy—period. There was a special menu for Christmas, but the waitress quickly started running down the list and telling us what they were out of.

It ended up with pancakes being the main delicacy being offered. We ordered them with hungry eyes and churning stomachs. They were fine. But halfway through the meal they ran out of tea. How can you run out of tea?

Never, ever again, will my house be so low on supplies. It was reasonable that we wouldn't want much on hand since we were leaving for Jekyll Island the next day for a week. But I have learned my lesson. I am stocking the shelves entirely. As Scarlett O'Hara swore while she clutched the radish in her fist, "As God is my witness, me and mine will never go hungry again!"

Half Way Home

My Friend, Julia Roberts

I am a Julia Roberts fan. Since she is a Georgia native she has a warm spot in my heart. Plus I have interviewed her a couple of times and have always found her to be nice and down to earth. When I heard she was coming to Perry to film the movie *Something To Talk About* I tried to line up another interview but didn't have any luck. Then a brainstorm hit me. I would sign on as an extra for the film and get to see Julia that way. I was sure as soon as she looked my way our eyes would meet, the thoughts would form, and viola! We would arrange to do lunch.

What a simple plan! How could it help but happen. So a few Saturdays ago I woke up at 4:30 A.M., got dressed, and headed out to have breakfast with some friends. From the restaurant we were going to the Ag Center to be extras in the Julia Roberts movie.

We arrived promptly at 6:00 A.M. and filled out all the necessary forms. There was quite a crowd of people there. The stands of the arena were almost filled. Those seats that were not taken by live bodies were filled with cardboard cutouts.

We got out instructions for the day from a Warner Brothers rep. She was cheerful, perky, and so glad we had all come out. Our "scene" was to involve watching Julia Roberts' movie daughter participate in a horse show. We were to eat hotdogs, drink soft drinks, and applaud on cue. My mind was saying over and over "I can do that! I can do that!"

Before the first scene was shot I was discovered. A Warner Brothers worker took me aside and told me I was going to be part of the background for the scene. That meant I was to walk when the director said action. I was to walk, get called to by Perry residents Richard and Rose May Smith, and go over and talk with them. Hey, did this guy know talent or what. Obviously my strong personality had made me stand out and be noticed.

But before the scene was shot, Richard and Rose May were noticed in a bigger way and were moved to sit in one of the cherished arena box seats. Now I had no one to holler to me and call me over. I had to improvise quickly and find a substitute caller. This turned out to be a lady named Marie. They called, "Action!" and I walked, reacted, and gave it my all. I was sure I would receive congratulations from the director, Lasse Halstrom. After all, he had raved over Holly Hunter's performance in his film *Once Around* and she was a fellow Georgian. But Lasse stayed put and no one said anything about my walk and talk.

From that moment on, nothing else special happened to me. I was back in the bleachers as one of the crowd. Others got to walk and act as individuals, but not me.

The day crawled on and I found myself getting more and more bored. Now you have to understand, I have a hard time sitting still in church for one hour, and this was sitting in the bleachers for hour after hour after hour. I got up and went to the restroom; I tried to strike up a variety of conversations with my co-stars; I tried to read a book. Nothing relieved the boredom.

Finally, it was lunchtime and we pushed our way to the food tables. We were all like salmon swimming upstream to spawn. I hope the salmon got a better reward for their efforts than we did. We were treated to Spam sandwiches and pink lemonade. So much for the Hollywood feast I expected.

Soon it was back to the bleachers. This time Robert Duval did make a brief appearance. And Julia was spotted at the far end of the stadium. I guess it was Julia. At that range, who could tell?

Getting desperate I made my way through the back hallways of the arena and came up close to where the actors were standing. It was Julia! She was dressed in a black outfit and had that wild mane of hair swinging about her shoulders. I cleared my throat. She turned around. Her face lifted toward me, and she looked right through me. Thud!

Then with a turn she was gone. I guess she had someone waiting for her outside. I went back to my seat. I finished the day and raced away from the arena. I had had my fill of being an extra. The day had ended with no Julia, no stardom, no fun.

One day I will interview my friend Julia Roberts again, and when I do I will tell her how she snubbed me in my hometown. I am sure she

Half Way Home

will be contrite, and after she begs my forgiveness a hundred times, then I will forgive her. Sure! In my dreams.

Another Set of Angels

One thing I stressed to my sons from the day they got their drivers' licenses was the importance of keeping your gas tank filled. Never let it get below a quarter of a tank, I admonished them, and that way you will never run out of gas. Good words to live by.

It's a shame I don't listen to my own wisdom. It would save me from a lot of problems. For instance, a few weeks ago on a Friday night I went to the movies. I got out of the theater around 6:45 P.M. and called my wife to tell her I was going to get gas and then head home.

Leaving the theater I headed for the nearest service station but its pumps were occupied. Looking at the gas gauge I saw that the little measuring arm was a fraction above the empty level. Since I know my car and it always carries a quarter of a tank of gas below the "empty" marking, I decided to make it to Byron.

Down the road I sped, without a care in the world. But then about five miles out from Byron the car sputtered. I couldn't imagine what was happening. Soon I knew because the car literally died. I couldn't believe it. I was so mad at that car I couldn't stand it.

I let the car glide over to the far side of the road and then got out and locked it. I figured the walk couldn't be too bad, especially since the rain that had been occurring earlier in the day had stopped. From my mind to God's ear! As soon as I had that thought the sky opened up and a downpour started. I had no umbrella and I was dressed in gray slacks, white shirt, tie and blazer. I was a sharp but soggy dresser.

Up ahead of me I saw a van had pulled off the road. I didn't want to be getting into any strange van, so I decided I would just walk around the street side of it and go on my merry way.

Just as I got behind the van the side door opened and the most bedraggled looking fellow I have ever seen stepped out. He looked like a refugee from the Charles Manson look-alike contest.

"What's the problem?" he asked.

"Nothing," I answered, still walking.

"Where are you going?" he now asked.

"Just to the next exit," I answered again.

"Get in and I'll give you a lift," he said with a smile.

"That's ok," I said. "I don't mind walking."

"No man, I'll give you a lift. It's raining bad," he insisted.

I honestly could not think of a reason not to get into the van though the voice inside was screaming, "Don't get in that van!" This was another thing I had always told my family. Never get into a strange vehicle.

As I go into this vehicle "Mr. Manson" pulled a lever and the door closed behind me.

As the vehicle started up he said, "I'm Ed and that is my friend Joe."

I looked behind me and there was a guy on a bed in the back of this vehicle. He waved his hand at me. He's probably the one with the knife I thought. He'll slit my throat and take my money. I knew he would be disappointed since I only had fifteen dollars on me.

In just a few minutes I saw the exit looming ahead of us. With relief I saw that Ed had his blinker on and was turning off the interstate.

As we pulled up to the service station Ed offered to take me back to my car. I thanked him but said that wasn't necessary as I could call my son. I handed him five dollars, which he didn't want to take, and stepped down from the van. Ed and Joe then sped off into the night.

I still advise people not to get into cars with strangers, and I still stress to my family not to get low on gas, but on this rainy night in Georgia my prayers were answered and I was rescued by two scruffy looking angels of mercy.

The Engagement

It is amazing how fast the time does go. It seems it was only a few days ago when my children were small and now they are all grown up. It is not only my own children being grown that amazes me, it is also my friends' children. This point was driven home a few days ago when I received a call from the daughter of two of my best friends.

She was calling to tell me she was engaged. Engaged? I thought maybe she was calling to tell me she had gotten braces. In my eyes she is still twelve or thirteen, but in reality she is twenty-one, and she's wonderful. I just hope this fiancé (whom I have not met) knows how wonderful she is.

But I have to admit he sounds pretty special. The two of them met last summer when they were both working at a resort. He was a waiter and she was a hostess. I take it, it was love almost at first sight. I tell you this because it relates to their engagement.

On the day he proposed he had sent this young lady flowers and on the card it said he would pick her up at 6:15. He arrived promptly—in a taxi! That was a little disconcerting for her but nothing terribly radical.

Off they went to their favorite restaurant where they had a great dinner. All through the dinner she thought he might pop the question and spring the ring, but he didn't! Finally after desert the maitre d' appeared and said their car was waiting.

When they exited the restaurant a limousine was waiting for them. It took them to the resort where they had worked the previous summer. The young lady was led to the spot where the boy had first spotted her. He asked her to sit down in the chair where she had been on that fateful day, and then he asked her to close her eyes.

When he told her she could open her eyes he had changed from his "date" shirt to the Hawaiian shirt he had worn as a waiter back during the summer. Then he knelt down at her feet and proposed. As the "Saturday Night Live" Church Lady used to say, "Now isn't that special!"

Hearing that story makes me realize that romance, charm, and goodness haven't all gone with the wind. There are still people who try to maintain images of kindness and pure emotion.

I wish this young couple all the best. Marriage at its best is the best; and at its worst, well I guess it is everything bad that can be. This young man being so romantic at the start sure does put him under a heavy burden to meet and match the proposal on every occasion in the future. But with that kind of imagination he is probably up to the task.

And when they get married I will be there to see this little girl walk down the aisle. Just thinking about such a day is hard for me to accept, and on the day I will probably still think it is a dream. She will make a beautiful bride, and that beauty is both inside and out. My friend, Stephanie, all grown up and soon to be married. I just can't believe it.

The Mouse that Roared

An ear-piercing scream rang out. It shattered the quiet of a typical workday at my office. One minute it was quiet and then there was that scream. It came from the office next door to us where there is a female worker who is about seven months pregnant. My first thought was that she must be having her baby, and that caused panic.

But it wasn't the scheduled baby that had caused the scream. It was a rat. The lady had spied one in her office and screamed to let the world know it. She had also let everyone in the next block know it.

She finally calmed down and things got back to normal in my office, while the hunt for the rat continued next door. I didn't worry that much about it. I figured it would stay over there and we would be out of harm, and rat's way.

Hah! It wasn't ten minutes before another yell was heard and this one was in my office. The mouse, as it was now being called, had scampered across the feet of one of my employees while she was working at the computer. Now that employee was sitting on top of one of the desks in our office in order to keep her feet off the floor.

While I was trying to calm her down the mouse attacked another worker. Ok, it didn't attack her, but it did stop at her desk and look up at her. That was enough. You would think a lion had stepped out of the jungle and was romping through the workplace.

After having a rest the mouse scooted into one of the back rooms. That room emptied except for me and one of my male workers. In a non-sexist workplace we had been elected to catch the mouse. That doesn't seem to be exactly fair but it sure is the way it lined up.

The mouse, when we saw it running behind desks and under air conditioner units, looked to be teeny. It wasn't Mickey size at all but seemed to be a miniature mouse. Of course, the women in my office acted like it was six feet long and had protruding fangs. One of them called out, "Watch it! Rats have slimy bodies and they can crawl right up the walls!" I really appreciated those comments as my one fear was that the mouse was going to run up my pants leg.

For the better part of an hour we tried to trap the mouse. I even had my coworker climb on top of a desk so he could drop a box over it when it moved from one place to the next. But the mouse was a speeder and could move more quickly than I ever imagined.

Finally, we did manage to get it trapped behind a box, and here the story gets sad. Tenderhearted people or members of the ASPCA may not want to know what happened next.

When we moved the box back the mouse was dead. Or he was a good actor and was playing possum. He lay sprawled on his back with his paws in the air. Death had come to our building.

I managed to get him picked up in some tissues and deposited him in my trashcan. I didn't relish picking him up but somebody had to do it and I was elected. Yuck!

Just before I left for the day I heard a little rustling in my trash can. Was it him? Who knows. Was I going to look? Are you crazy? I figure the janitorial crew could have some of the fun we had had during the day. And maybe little Mickey could escape from them and live happily ever after.

The Gift of Time

A few weeks ago my youngest son and his girlfriend took a one-day trip to South Carolina to visit my parents. It was spring break and they decided this was something they wanted to do. It wasn't my idea. It was theirs. If I had suggested it they would have probably would have said no, but since it was their idea it was okay.

Anyway they drove the four hours to South Carolina, had lunch with my folks, toured the town, visited some at their home, and then drove four hours back. Amazingly, when they got back they talked about what a good time they had.

Clinton, South Carolina, where I grew up and where my parents still reside, is a pretty city. Presbyterian College is located there, as is Thornwell Orphanage. When I was growing up I knew a lot of kids who lived at Thornwell and to my mind, aside from a traditional home, they had the best thing.

Anyway Sean and Paula were much impressed with the orphanage as well as the college. They also loved the old homes that are located there. One of my best friends in high school lived in one of these big homes and it is still as elegant today as it was then. It is a traditional Southern structure with wide columns and big porches and big, big rooms. They don't build them like this anymore.

After they toured this metropolis of 10,000 citizens they went to a local steak house for something to eat. Then it was over to my cousin Lynn's home to meet some relatives. Lynn is a car dealer and this family-owned business has been there forever. I see cars on the streets of Georgia that have "Lynn Cooper Motors" tags on the front. He is a major wheeler/dealer in the car arena. He and the members of his immediate family also own a dress shop, an interior design office, and many homes and apartments which he rents. He is the rich side of the family.

When the visit with the kin-people was over my folks and their visitors went home and spent the rest of their time looking at old yearbooks and photographs. I think that is what people always do when they visit older relatives.

A few days after Sean and Paula got back to Perry my stepmother called me. She just wanted me to know how wonderful they were on their trip. She said they were so well behaved and so loving and courteous. These of course are words every parent wants to here.

Before she hung up my stepmother added, "You know it is so wonderful when young people want to spend time with older people I know there were other things they would have rather done but they spent time with us, and we really love them for it."

I guess the older we get the more we appreciate time spent on us and with us. And it is such an easy gift. Time doesn't cost anything. It is adjustable. And it is just about always greatly appreciated. Maybe more of us should practice giving this simple gift. If my folks reaction was any criteria, the "visit" was worth its weight in gold.

Jury Duty

It is not uncommon for people to react to a notice for jury duty like it was a summons for a root canal. Any possible excuse usually crosses the receiver's mind and elaborate escape plots are formulated. But in the end, most people end up grinning and bearing it like I did last week.

For the majority of my adult life I was immune to these summons. I was a practicing attorney for several years, and after that the Georgia rules were that attorneys, whether practicing or not, would not serve on juries. But that ended and I got on the list.

In my years of practicing law I dealt at first with real estate law and later with military law. In both instances I never participated in a jury trail.

Last week when I reported to court in Perry I was ready to study this American process in more detail. I was especially interested since watching the O. J. Simpson trial. Those jurors have had maximum exposure of the anonymous kind. And after the trial ends, watch out! They will be major celebrities.

When I arrived at the courthouse I signed in with the clerk's office and then headed upstairs to the courtroom. I was a little surprised to see a metal detector in place. I think it was a good idea, but I just didn't know it was used in the entrance to the courtroom.

At 9:00 A.M. on the nose Judge George Nunn entered the court. Now I have known George for years, but in this situation and in "his" court I wasn't entirely sure how to act. Should I wave and shout "Hi, George" or just ignore him until addressed by him? And when I respond should he be called "Judge" or "George"?

During the first day, the issue of name-calling didn't arise. I caught George's eye and gave him a smile of recognition. He did the same. Before we had the opportunity to address each other, my name was called to move to another courtroom. It seems there were two trials being handled simultaneously.

Now I was in Judge Buster McConnell's court. Here we were each asked to stand and give some information about ourselves. Another crisis. How detailed should I be? Should I say my name after it was called or just stand up and start talking? These are some serious questions that were going through my mind.

Buster did a lot to alleviate a tense situation. He joked with some of the people, not in a way that took away the seriousness of our purpose in being there, but enough to put the "potential jurors" at ease. The lawyers who were representing the parties to the divorce case also were fairly relaxed.

I made my statement as to employment, etc., and sat down. I thought I had been forthright, but brief—just what was appropriate. Right or wrong, it was now in the hands of the lawyers. They looked us all over. They made their preemptive strikes and I was not chosen.

After all my annoyance at having to serve on jury duty, now I was angered by being dismissed once again so casually. What did I say wrong? What did I do wrong? I was full of doubts about my personality and my appearance. I was not one of the chosen.

Now I thought I would be dismissed. I had given it my best shot and I had not been selected. It was time to pay me my money and send me home. That didn't happen.

I was under the wrong impression that when you reported for jury duty, and you were not selected you were excused. Wrong! If there is more than one trial scheduled during the session you have to take your chances on being selected for any jury during the week. So when I was not selected for the trial being held in Judge Buster McConnell's court I was sent back to Judge George Nunn's court to see if I could be chosen for the next trial.

Somehow by just watching the lawyers and seeing how they looked at us and the questions they asked, I knew I was going to be selected. I also felt the woman next to me was. Guess what? We both were. Call it male intuition.

Once our names were called and we were sent to sit in a jury box we became a unit. It was amazing how fast that happened. It was like going to summer camp, the friendships were made quickly and deeply.

This feeling of being "us" instead of "I" intensified as we listened to the opening arguments.

When we had been sitting as "non-jurors" and listening and watching the rituals of the court, I had heard comments made about one lawyer's shoes looking scruffy. Another comment was that one of their suits didn't fit well. Of such are first impressions made.

The lawyers must be aware of how these slight prejudices can play in a case because one of them actually said, "If I do or say any thing to offend you as a juror, please hold it against me but don't take it out on my client."

The opening arguments were brief and soon we were in the jury deliberation room while the lawyers tried to reach agreement on some points of law. This deliberation room is the type of place where the O. J. Simpson jury has spent most of their days. There has been little actual time in the courtroom.

In the deliberation room we were asked not to talk about the case so we spent our time getting to know each other better. You would be surprised how much you can learn in one brief two-hour period. There were no books to read in there, no television set to watch, so there was noting to do but talk. And talk we did.

Finally, we were allowed to break for lunch. Upon our return we were told the case had been settled. For some it was a relief while for others it was a disappointment. I think all of us were psychologically ready to try the case.

Judge Nunn was very kind in thanking us for our participation. He let us know that he knew we had all been willing to do our duty. Plus, we got fifteen dollars a day for our troubles.

Maybe one of these days I will actually go through a trial from start to finish as a juror. And then again maybe not. But having seen the process in action I do have a lot of respect for the people who give up their time to be jurors. Most get into the swing of things and become dedicated. After all that is the American way.

I Remember Mama (Mother)

Whenever I get the chance, I talk or write about my mother. Although she died when I was fourteen, she made an impact that lasts until this day. It amazes me how much I remember about her and how many funny, interesting stories there are to tell.

One of my favorite days with my mother was on my eighth birthday. It was a Saturday and she told me that as my gift I could spend the day any way I wanted. That included sleeping late. I think I probably got out of bed on that day around noon. I have always hated to go to bed at night and have always hated getting up in the morning.

Anyway, when I got up she and I headed downtown. I did not include my brother in this excursion. He stayed home. And my father was working, so he didn't get to go either. It was just me and my mother. She was mine exclusively for the day.

My mother asked where I wanted to eat lunch and I chose Howard's Pharmacy. This was back in the days when drugstores had luncheon counters. We ordered ham sandwiches and fountain cokes. Since those days of my childhood, I have never had a ham sandwich that tasted like those did at Howard's Pharmacy. They were toasted with the edges cut off the bread. The sandwich was made up of ham, mustard, and mayonnaise. Two pickles sat on top.

I think I had two or three of these sandwiches and possibly two or more cokes. It was wonderful. One of the top meals of my life.

After the feast we went to the movie at the Broadway Theater. We saw a western. I don't remember who the cowboy was but Yvonne DeCarlo (who later gained fame as TV's "Lily Munster") was the cowboy's girlfriend. I am sure my mother just loved the movie.

Following the movie we went shopping and I got to pick out my present. I don't recall anything about what I picked, but I'm sure it was great since the whole day lives in my memory as one of my very best.

Another short memory of my Mother is when I was in the sixth grade. On the last day of school your parents came to pick you up.

Most of the fathers were working, so it was mostly the mothers who came.

Carolyn McDaniel and I came down the hall together to where our mothers were standing. We handed them our report cards. My mother said in an excited voice, "Jackie made all A's." Carolyn's mother said just as excitedly, "Carolyn passed!"

It always impressed me how happy Mrs. McDaniel was with the "passing." To me that was true Mother love.

Finally, I always liked to hear my mother sing. She had a pretty voice, not exceptional but full of emotion. She would use this emotion to sing ballads about misguided love and faithless lovers. She knew all the words, and if she didn't know them she made some good ones up.

I would beg her to sing the saddest songs over and over. And she would. Through the years since her death, more than anything I have missed the sound of her songs.

Mel Gibson

There are big celebrities in Hollywood and there are little celebrities in Hollywood. It depends on the time of the year and the impact of their last movie as to how big they are at any given time. But some stars are stars and always attract interest. For me a true star is Elizabeth Taylor. What I wouldn't give for a chance to meet her!

A lot of people must consider Mel Gibson a biggie. At least judging by the reaction I got among my friends when I announced I was interviewing Mel in connection with his film *Braveheart*. They were all impressed. And the women were gaga.

Never have I had so many offers to help me record the interview, drive up with me to Atlanta, or take notes in shorthand or longhand. I could have taken an entire bus full of women with me and still have left disappointed ones at home.

Now that I have been to Mel and back, let me dismiss some of the myths about him. He is not five-foot-two as many have speculated. He's about five-foot-ten, and, ok, maybe he does wear lifts in his shoes. He also is American born though he moved with his family at an early age to Australia.

He's married and has six kids. He takes them on location with him whenever possible. He does not want any of them to be child actors. He also is not a very good disciplinarian. He would rather be the good, fun guy and let his wife take care of the authoritarian stuff. "They listen when their mother speaks," he said, "but then I listen when she speaks."

The strange thing about interviewing Mel was how much alike we are. I never knew that. I mean, we must be physically alike because when we were side by side people would come up and address me as Mel and ask for my autograph. Then other people were asking him if he was "Jackie Cooper." I guess it is because we both have blue eyes.

Most of our time was spent discussing *Braveheart*, his new action epic based on the life of Scottish hero William Wallace. Gibson not only stars in the movie, he also directed it. "It all has to do with getting the money for a movie," he said with a grin. "In order to get financing you have to have a bankable star. Me being the director wasn't enough. Me being in it meant I could get the financing to get it made, so I cast myself as the star."

Statements like this are made without the slightest bit of conceit. It's just an awareness of who he is and what he does. He makes movies and they make money—that makes him bankable.

I reminded him there are plans to remake one of his earliest movies, *Tim*. He co-starred with Piper Laurie in this movie back in the early 1970s. "I'm only thirty-nine and they are already doing re-makes. That is weird!"

Before I left Atlanta I asked for an autograph. Mel Gibson must have been a medical student at some point in his life because the signature is totally unreadable scrawl. But it's Mel's. I'm going to have it framed because as I was told by so many people—"He's a biggie!"

A Disney Celebration

The Walt Disney Company graciously invited me to attend a press junket in New York last week. The reason for the junket was the new Disney animated film *Pocahontas*. Several of the stars, animators, directors, and musicians would be available for interview during the three days of the junket.

I would be in New York for three days, Tuesday through Thursday, and I was asked if I would like to stay over for the big "Picnic in Central Park" where 100,000 people would watch *Pocahontas* on giant screens. I don't like heat and I don't like crowds so as far as I was concerned there would be 99,999 at the picnic.

Right before I left to drive up to Atlanta to catch my plane, my son J. J. asked if he could use my car to drive to Columbus, Ohio, where he was going on vacation. Being the good father that I am, I said, "Sure." This left me driving to Atlanta in J. J.'s Hyundai, which has a stick shift, and an air conditioner system that doesn't work.

Still, I made the flight on time and was soon winging my way to New York, or rather to New Jersey. For some reason I had been booked into the Newark airport rather than one of the New York ones. I asked the guy seated next to me how far Newark was from New York City and he said it was only over the river. But he did say he hoped I had a lot of cash on me since the cab ride usually ran about forty-five to fifty dollars. That would cut it close since I had sixty dollars in cash.

After the plane landed, I was stopped by a clean-cut looking man in a coat and tie who asked if I needed information about rides. I figured he was with the airport information service so I asked him about shuttles. He said the shuttle took about two hours and cost thirty-five to forty dollars. He said a cab would be that much or more, though quicker.

He said there was a limousine service that ran about forty dollars that went directly to the hotel where I was staying. I said that sounded good and he told me to go out front of the airport and I would be picked up. I went out front, a limousine drove up, and the clean-cut man was the driver.

He threw my bags in the trunk and invited me to sit up front with him. And off we went. The guy was amazing. He knew a little bit about everything. We went through Bayonne, New Jersey, and then to Hoboken and he gave me a quick history of each town. Then we headed into the Holland Tunnel and he told me all about its construction.

When we reached New York City he asked if I was in a rush to get to the hotel. I said, "No," but I wondered why he would ask that. He said that if I had time he would show me some of the city. It's bad, but I was a little suspicious of why he would offer to do that. I thought this might cost me a bundle, but he hadn't mentioned cost, so I said, "Ok."

This guy took me by the Statue of Liberty, the United Nations Building, the World Trade Center where the bomb blast was, the Battery, and several other landmark places. And he didn't charge me one extra penny. It was amazing. Then he deposited me at the Regency Hotel and took off.

I guess there are good people everywhere. You just have to luck into them. This man did say that he was coming to Jekyll Island in two weeks to see his niece get married. I hope the people down there are as hospitable to him as he was to me.

The Regency Hotel, where he deposited me, is an old but attractive hotel in the Wall Street area. As soon as I got there I checked out my room—it was great!—and then went out to explore the sidewalks of New York.

I went down a few blocks and headed west. I passed places like the Trump Tower, Armani's and other elite fashion establishments. Just as I was within a block of the Plaza Hotel I noticed the guy walking next to me. We were almost walking in lockstep. As I looked over I realized that I knew him, or at least I recognized him.

I kept trying to place who it was, and just as he turned and started into the Plaza I realized it was Jason Gould, the Jason Gould who played Barbara Streisand's son in *The Prince of Tides* and who is her son in real life.

Only when someone later told me they had seen Larry King near the Plaza did it dawn on me that he was interviewing Streisand on his tenth anniversary show from the Plaza. I guess Jason was with his mama in New York.

When I got back to the hotel from my walk it was time to go to the screening of *Pocahontas*. The critics gathered together and tromped over to the theater where it was being shown. The theater was packed and everyone was excited about seeing Disney's latest animated classic.

When you see the film be sure to watch through the credits in order to hear the pop versions of some of the Alan Mencken/Stephen Swartz songs. Jon Secada and Shaneice sing "If I Never Knew You" and Vanessa Williams sings "Colors of the Wind."

After the movie a group of us went back to the Regency to eat a late supper. This was a pretty swanky place, and it seemed to insult our waiter that we all wanted separate checks. I mean, he almost refused. He came as close to saying "no way" as he could without saying "absolutely not." Why this is such a problem I don't know.

After the meal I went up to my room for a good night's sleep. I put my key in the lock, and it wouldn't turn. I checked to make sure it was the right room and then tried again. It still wouldn't work. I tried and tried and tried and tried. Nothing! I was locked out. So down to the lobby I went.

The concierge sent one of the hotel's employees upstairs with me and he worked on the lock. Finally, he got the door open. He asked if I was going back out that night. When I said no, he said a locksmith would be up the next morning to fix it.

The next morning I sat in my room and waited for the locksmith to arrive. When he hadn't come by 10:00 A.M. I went out to look around New York some more. When I got back, you guessed it, the lock wouldn't work. It was back downstairs with the same complaint. This time they located a locksmith and sent him back up with me. He fixed the door.

By now it was time for the series of interviews I had scheduled with the men and women behind *Pocahontas*. I was feeling pretty energetic as I started the marathon of interviews the Disney people set up for the junket. But even people as lively as I am can get worn down after interviewing animators, directors, and stars for hours on end.

We were all escorted to a downtown hotel where tables (probably about fifteen) had been set up. Four or five members of the press sat at each table and the celebrities rotated to us. Pity the poor "stars," they had to endure table after table of people asking the same questions over and over.

Of all the people we talked with my favorites were Glen Keane, Judy Kuhn, and Alan Menken. Glen Keane is the artist/animator who brought the character of Pocahontas to life. He also gave us "Ariel": the Little Mermaid, and "Belle": the Beauty of Beauty and the Beast.

Keane is the son of the artist who draws "The Family Circus." That is the cartoon that appears in the comic section of the paper, and Keane is in there as one of the children. Now Glen Keane says his son is getting into animation and drawing of all kinds. I guess the torch will be passed to him one day.

I have been talking with Glen Keane on and off since *The Little Mermaid* days and he is as nice as anyone can be. His niceness obviously hasn't been a handicap as *Premiere* magazine recently named him one of the 100 most powerful people in Hollywood. I am glad to see he is finally getting recognized for his talent.

Judy Kuhn is recognized mainly for her voice. In the film *Pocahontas* she is the singing voice of the Indian Princess and gets to warble "Just around the Riverbend" and "Colors of the Wind." Her voice is simply beautiful and the lady in real life is as pretty as her voice.

What impressed me about Kuhn was how family oriented she is. She and her husband have a new daughter (their first child) and Kuhn says she just can't get interested in going back to work on Broadway. She says her daughter is so fascinating she wants to spend every minute of the day with her. And I bet the kid loves hearing her mother sing the *Pocahontas* songs.

Then there is Alan Menken. What a great guy he is, and so talented. He has written the music for *Little Mermaid, Beauty and the Beast, Aladdin*, and *Pocahontas*. Years ago he and his then-partner

Howard Ashman created the songs for *Little Shop of Horrors*. Ashman died of AIDS a few years back but Menken is always quick to mention him and his talent in any interview he gives.

People who can compose music fascinate me. I guess it is just so alien to anything I can do. Just imagine being able to sit down and let music flow from you. And it flows from Menken in torrents.

I asked how his family liked having somebody at home who can provide music on demand. He laughed and said his wife was always telling him to quit playing the piano because he was going to wake up the baby. I told him just to come on down to Perry, and I would rent a piano and he could play to his heart's content—and mine.

There were a lot of other people to talk with in New York but these three were the best. I am always amazed when "celebrities" are ordinary people with extraordinary talents, and many of them are. They could be the same people you talk to in your town, at your job, or in your church. They just happen to have mega-talents.

The next event from Disney was a picnic in the park for the press. They sat up big tents and served delicious food. A few days later there would be a "Picnic in the Park" for everyone who came to the *Pocahontas* premiere, but the one I went to was just for the press and it was a much smaller event.

I found myself at a table with a group of people from South Africa. They had come over to do a television story on the happenings. A nicer bunch of people I have never met, and one of them was a beautiful woman named Bussy. While talking to them I found out she was Miss South Africa and runner-up to Miss World. Wow!

The next morning I flew out of New Jersey early and headed back south. I arrived in Atlanta just a little before noon. It was the hottest part of the day on a very hot day. As I carried my suit bag out to the parking lot I almost melted into the ground. Finally, I spied my son's Hyundai which I had driven.

I raced to it. I put the key in the door. I slid into the seat. I put the key in the ignition and turned. Nothing! I had left the lights on when I parked two days before. The battery was deader than dead. I marveled at my stupidity.

Now what do you do when you have a dead battery at the Atlanta airport and no jumper cables? Well, you scream a lot. And you sweat even more. Then you walk down to the area where you pay your parking fees and ask for help. And you get it. The lady was as nice as could be. She asked which row I was parked in, told me to put up my hood, and said there would be a twenty dollar fee.

I staggered back to my car, put up the hood, and luckily found a tree to sit under while I waited. It took about thirty minutes for the repairman to get there and about fifteen seconds to get the car started. It was the best twenty dollars I ever spent.

By now it was going on one o'clock in the afternoon and it was hotter than hot. The air conditioner in my son's car did not work so I was steaming as I drove. I wanted to stop and get something to drink but I was afraid to stop the car. I thought it might not start back. So down the interstate I went, hot, humid, and thirsty.

I am what is known as a high sweater. Some people perspire. Pigs and I sweat. I had a band of moisture across my chest from where the seat belt crossed. It was like a small river. I kept expecting to see fish in it.

Cars passed by me with their windows rolled up and their air conditioning going full blast. I did not have kind thoughts for them. My glasses were steamed, my hair was wet, my disposition was the pits.

Finally, I made it to Macon and to my son's apartment. As I pulled in I knew that I had made it into the "Fatherhood Hall of Fame." I should be bronzed and put on display. Flowers should be left at my feet.

I threw the keys toward him, grabbed the ones for my car, and left. I turned on the air conditioner full blast. It was heaven.

A few days later my son bought a new car. It seems driving mine around while I was gone made him appreciate air conditioning. I can't wait to borrow it.

There are a few creature comforts I can take or leave. Air conditioning, I have found, is not one of them.

Emani

Let me say it one more time, I hate to fly. But fly I do, and a lot. Once I have landed and have kissed the ground, I am okay. At least until the next time I have to get on a plane. What I mean is I have no remaining negative effects. A few weeks ago I had a trip scheduled to Los Angeles. My flight was supposed to leave Atlanta at noon, putting me into Los Angeles at three. I had made arrangements for a friend to meet my plane and everything else was settled.

I had my first inkling of problems when I arrived at the airport. By the time I left the main terminal and got to the gate where my plane was supposed to be, they had changed the gate. Then a few minutes later a sign went up saying the flight was delayed. Rumor was there was an engine problem.

We finally got on the plane at one o'clock. I was sitting in the very back of the plane. The person seated next to me turned out to be a three-year-old little girl. As soon as she sat down she asked, "What's your name?"

I answered her and she said, "I'm Emani."

Her mother quickly reached over and turned Emani's face toward hers. "Emani," she asked, "what have I told you about talking to strangers." Emani quickly responded, "This isn't a stranger. This is Jackie."

Her mother spoke again insistently, "No Emani, what did I tell you about strangers?"

Emani solemnly answered. "Strangers will run over you."

Her mother hid a smile and answered gently, "No, Emani, you are confusing strangers and cars."

While we sat on the ground waiting to taxi out Emani kept me entertained with a variety of topics. She was charming, intelligent and the most loveable little girl I have been around in some time. She was only three, but she was three going on thirty.

Our plane finally taxied out to the runway to take off, but it didn't stay in line very long. Before I knew it we were headed back to the departure gate. It seems there was something wrong with the air conditioning. And they were right because that plane got hot fast.

For the next forty minutes we sat at the gate and sweltered. They even opened the side doors to let air in. And all through the ordeal Emani's good nature never left her. She was wonderful.

Finally, they told us they couldn't get it fixed and we would have to deplane. Other arrangements to get to Los Angeles would have to be made. Emani and her mother were very concerned since they lived in L. A. and really needed to get back.

We said our goodbyes and they rushed off to try to locate another flight. I hung around the desk and waited to see if any alternative routes would be offered. In about ten minutes they announced we should move to another gate because another plane had been found to transport us.

We were told to keep our same assigned seats. So when I got to mine I found that Emani and her mother were not there. I really didn't expect them since I figured they had made other arrangements. But just before they closed the doors I heard a voice call out from the aisle, "Jackie, I'm back!"

Takeoffs are my very least favorite part of flying. So usually I tense my hands, grip the armrests, and close my eyes. This I did as the plane lifted off. With my eyes closed I felt a small hand on my arm. I looked down into her sweet face and she said, "Jackie, I'm here for you."

And she was, all the way to L. A. I have tried to forget the delayed flight and all its problems, but I will always remember Emani.

Half Way Home

Heat Wave

We are really having a heat wave. I mean it is hot! Has it ever been so hot before? Not in my memory, that's for sure. These days I sit in my air-conditioned office, drive home in my air-conditioned car, and stay put in my air-conditioned house. I do not venture outside for anything more than food. For food I do brave the heat.

Heat to me is the most debilitating of the elements. I can get warm when I am cold by adding more clothes but with heat there is only so much you can take off. And I take off as much as I can as quickly as I can. Someone once said if I got in a traffic jam on the way home from work I would be arrested for indecent exposure.

My stripping to a pair of shorts completely aggravates my wife. She is of the school that says men should wear shirts just as women are required to do. When I venture outside shirtless she is offended. When I come to the table to eat a meal without a shirt, she is horrified.

I do have to admit that sometimes covering my huge white body might be a good idea. Case in point. The other afternoon I was home alone and the back doorbell rang. It was the usual time that the Federal Express man makes deliveries. Dressed in a pair of shorts, I threw open the backdoor expecting to have a package handed to me. Instead it was the mother of one of the ladies in my movie class.

Poor woman, I think she was blinded by my whiteness. I also think she decided "Freewilly" was on the loose. In any event she probably nearly wrecked her car on the way home since her eyesight had been damaged by the glare.

When I related this occurrence to my wife, she was horrified. Once again I got Lecture 101 on proper social attire. This time I did listen more attentively.

It guess it all goes back to my childhood. Back in those days prior to air conditioning (Yes, I am that old.) we spent our lives in khaki pants. When the weather got warm we were even allowed to go to school barefooted. At least the boys were. I don't remember the girls having bare feet.

All the houses had screened-in side porches where you could sit and usually catch a breeze. At night you kept the windows wide open and the beds were usually in a corner between two of them. On the hottest of nights my folks put up a fan in the window to draw in the air.

During the hottest part of the day during the summer months we had to stay inside. That was between twelve and two. It was called naptime but usually it consisted of playing Monopoly or some other board game. A lot of times though my brother would actually go to sleep, which used to irk the dickens out of me.

The point is that life did go on in those days. We may not have had air-conditioned homes or cars but we did cope. We may have gone around half-naked but we did cope.

Old habits die hard and that's why I act the way I do today.

Pat Conroy

Whenever I get a spare minute I read. And lately I have been reading nothing but great novels. I love to read and usually have a book going at all times, and some of them are good and some of them are bad. Odds are you will get a better than average story about one out of every four. The past few weeks I have beaten that average and then some.

If you haven't read John T. Lescoart's *A Certain Justice*, Danielle Steele's *Lightning*, Ken Follett's *A Place Called Freedom* or John J. Nance's *Pandora's Clock* then you don't know what good reading is. Still the best thing I have read lately is Pat Conroy's *Beach Music*.

Conroy is a particular favorite of mine. He isn't a prolific writer but he's a great one. I first discovered him with *The Lords of Discipline*, a novel that recounted some of his experiences at The Citadel in Charleston, South Carolina. Having been raised in South Carolina I was interested in any fiction that came out about that state. And Conroy perfectly captured the feel of the South and the love/hate relationship many of us have with it.

Next came *The Prince of Tides*. This was vintage Conroy and brought him a wider audience than anyone expected. I lost that exclusive feeling about his work and became one of thousands who thrived on his word phrasings as well as his storytelling abilities. There were parts of *Tides* that were so beautifully written that they could be called a form of freestyle poetry.

Once again the setting was South Carolina and once again I had the feeling I had lived some of the experiences he described. My hometown of Clinton, South Carolina, had some of the eccentricities he observed, and some of the traumas of my life were somewhat akin to his.

I read recently that Conroy said a writer could not be blessed with anything better than a dysfunctional family. Well, I don't call my family dysfunctional per se, but I think there is a lot of fodder for writing in there that Conroy could use. Like him I adored my mother, and like him I lost her to a cruel disease. The difference is he lost his late in life while I lost mine early on.

He has said he got his love of the English language from his mother. She was the one who inspired him to write. From mine I got the thought of being "special." That is what she told me every day of my life for the fourteen years we shared together. Both women gave gifts to their sons that they have always used.

A friend of mine told me recently that we are all living Conroy stories. That really hit home to me. I can imagine him observing my life and getting several novels from it. He could write about my early years when life was almost perfect and I breezed through the days with almost no cares. Then he can have the serpent entering my Garden of Eden through my mother's illness and death that uprooted my calm and changed my life forever.

The next book can be about my life with my stepmother and how we did not communicate. How my father tried to be the referee between us and never succeeded. This book would be the most depressing and probably the longest.

In the third novel of this trilogy he could write about redemption. This would be the most optimistic of the three and would show how things do get better for those who wait. It would be a story of love, hope, and reconciliation.

So whenever Pat Conroy runs out of ideas he can come on down to Middle Georgia and have lots of material for his next 100 books. I'm ready for that visit whenever he is.

Grumpy Old Me

My birthday was last week. I couldn't believe it got here so quickly. They sure seem to come around with greater frequency than they used to. Or is that another sign that I'm getting older? Add to that my lack of people's responses when I tell my age. "Why you certainly don't look it!" they say. They might as well be saying, "I thought you were older than that!"

As I get older I get grumpier too. By the time a few more years have passed I will be a regular curmudgeon like Andy Rooney of "60 Minutes" fame. I'll be griping and groaning about everything.

My main gripe lately is the appearance of small children everywhere. I have raised my two boys and they are grownups. They haven't given me any grandchildren yet so I'm in that "not around small children" stage. When you are at this stage your tolerance level runs low.

Example number one: My wife and I went to Warner Robins a few nights ago to have a nice, quiet dinner. It was a Saturday and we had both had hard weeks so we were deserving of some peace and quiet. I told the hostess that we wanted "nonsmoking." I should have added "no children."

The table behind us was occupied by a family of four: father, mother, and two children under the age of five. Some idiot had given the two children balloons. The little girl was right behind my head and she stood and rubbed that balloon constantly. Not only was that an irritating sound, but I was ready at any moment for the balloon to pop and burst my eardrums.

The parents were oblivious to my discomfort. They were too busy screaming at the little boy to eat his food. They hollered and threatened for a good fifteen minutes. I thought I might turn around and tell him about the starving hordes in China and see if that would help but I held my tongue and kept listening for the thraack of the balloon.

Needless to say, we didn't have a great time at the restaurant. It didn't matter that the food was good; the atmosphere was the pits.

Example number two: I was at the movie recently. Since I can't make it through any film without a good supply of popcorn, I have to stand in however long a line there is and get my treat. The line on this day must have been fifteen people deep. And it was moving slowly.

My movie started at five minutes after seven and at seven o'clock I finally got to within one person of placing my order. The bad thing was that the person in front of me was a candidate for father of the year, or at least thought he was.

When he finally got to the front of the line, rather than place his order, he turned to his very small daughter and said, "Tell them what you want, honey."

The child just stared at him. He asked her again, and then again. Finally, she said she wanted the special children's treat of popcorn, candy, and a drink. The clerk got the popcorn and candy and then asked about the drink.

"What do you want to drink, honey?" asked father. Again he was met with silence (except for the heavy breathing of those of us behind him).

Not getting an answer, he proceeded to read off the names of all the drinks available to her. And with each word he spoke he turned and smiled at all of us behind him. He didn't get many smiles back.

Finally, some brave soul in the back of the line hollered out, "Move it up there!" The picture perfect father reddened and ordered the drink, picked up the order and his daughter, and moved away from the counter. I'm sure he was incensed that some idiot would be so rude.

No, the idiot was in front of me. There is a time and a place for the instructing of children on how to order from the concession stand. This time and place was not it.

Mary

Many years ago I heard a song titled "There's a Chapter in My Life Called Mary." I liked the idea of people and relationships being chapters in our lives. A few days ago I thought about this song title again because a chapter of my life called Mary was closed.

My parents called me to tell me that Mary Trammell had died. Mary Trammell was their next door neighbor and had been a friend of my family since time began. I had never known Clinton, South Carolina, not to be a place where Mary lived and it will be difficult for me to accept the fact that when I go "home" Mary will not be there.

My family moved to Holland Street when I was very small. I don't know my exact age at the time we moved, but I do know the things that occurred before that move are totally fuzzy in my mind. I do recall that even before we moved to our house on Holland Street, we had lived on that same street in a rented apartment. So we had been "on Holland Street" for some time.

Mary and Henry Trammell owned the house behind ours and it faced Stonewall Street. They were there when we moved in and were there when I moved away. They had two sons, Billy and Keith, who were a little younger than my brother and I.

The Trammells were the most compatible of neighbors. I can't remember a single fuss or disagreement between the two families in all the years we have been in the neighborhood. We even got along during the time we shared a telephone party line, and that really takes cooperation.

The extra treat we got from living next to Mary was that she baked cakes, and they were delicious cakes. For our birthdays Mary always made a special one (chocolate for me) and it was the highlight of the day. If you were really lucky she let you lick the batter bowl and the icing bowl.

From the earliest time that I knew her, I called Mary by her first name. I know some people would think I was being disrespectful, but is just wasn't that way. We called all my parents closest friends by their first names. And no one to my knowledge was offended. Now I know my wife would have a fit if my sons called our friends by their first names without preceding it by Mr. or Miss as in Miss Susan or Mr. Bill. But at the time and in that place we called Mary and Henry by their first names and it was perfectly acceptable.

Mary was a friend to my mother and to my stepmother. During my mother's illness and death she was a constant comfort and a link to the stability of the past. That link is perhaps what made her death so hard for me. She more than anyone else was my connection to those childhood days when it was always sunny and always happy.

Plus, Mary never changed. In my mind's eye she was ageless and she actually seemed not to age. The last time I saw her she still looked just like Mary should.

Yes, there was a chapter in my life called Mary. Now it has ended but for the rest of my life the memory will linger.

Just Drive the Car

Since I seem to be spending more and more time flying lately, and liking it less, here are some more thoughts on the subject.

Some of the things I did like about flying are being lost. For example, I always appreciated the fact that flying can get you just about anywhere faster than any other mode of transportation. However, a month or so ago I had to make a quick trip out to Los Angeles and back and it took me fourteen hours to get there due to the plane having problems.

Second example, I love airplane food. I eat everything they throw at me and beg for more. I have always had a fondness for their beef platters, and liked the second choice of chicken. On my last few flights I have been offered nothing but vegetarian lasagna. Yukkk!

I eat it like a good flyer, but do I like it? No! It is the most rubbery, non-tasting, excuse for food you have ever encountered. But it is all you are offered, not just one of the choices.

Third example, usually I am near the front of the airplane and can get off and get home in nothing flat. Except now there seems to be this problem with airplanes finding parking spaces. The last two times I have flown, my plane has had to wait on the runway when it landed because someone else was in its gate.

Now don't these people phone ahead and say they are on the way? And doesn't someone realize that if a plane full of people is coming into gate four, then whoever is in that spot had better get out of the way? Hey, duh, two and two equals four.

Another gripe is limousine drivers. Ok, I know that has nothing to do with flying but on my last three trips I have been met by a limousine. The company I am flying for provides them, so it doesn't come out of my pocket.

I always wanted to know who the people were in those tinted glass, humongous cars, and now I know—it's me. Anyway, my complaint is not with the cars but with the drivers. When I get in the car I want to sit quietly and think about my day, or how I was just spared by God one more time while being in an airplane.

Most drivers thinks I need friendship and companionship, or they wants to tell me the story of their lives. Honestly, on a recent trip the driver bent my ear for a full forty-five minutes about how he had lost his job at a bank and was reduced to driving a limo.

He also added in that his girlfriend of eight years had just left him. Plus, his father had cancer and was in the hospital having chemotherapy and the family was going bankrupt. And his sister had just gotten a divorce and she and her six-year-old son had moved back home. The only one having any luck was his younger brother who was in college studying to be a gynecologist but lately he had begun to act stupid and was making C's instead of A's.

Now I heard all of that in one short drive. By the time we reached the airport I was ready for the plane to drop out of the sky and onto this guy's head. He needed a therapist. I needed six aspirins.

Flying is getting worse; the limo drivers are getting suicidal. I think I had better just stay home.

My Life Is A Sitcom

Every once in a while I feel like my life is a situation comedy. Some days it is "Leave it to Beaver," other days it is "Ozzie and Harriet" and a few days ago it was "I Love Lucy." The only problem is that I was more like Lucy and my wife had the Ricky Ricardo role.

Ok, let me explain. It started when I stayed home sick from work. I had an upset stomach and didn't feel like facing the workday. After my wife left for work, I got up and took my medicine. Then I decided I needed something in my stomach. This isn't because I wasn't supposed to take the medicine without eating; it is because I have this theory that you eat normally even when your stomach is upset.

If you eat normal food, then your stomach doesn't get the idea there is anything wrong with it and it recovers. I know that is faulty logic, but it is my logic just the same.

So I went out and got a steak biscuit, some orange juice, and a large coffee. I also got my copies of *The Macon Telegraph* and *USA Today*. I was set for the morning.

I put the orange juice, coffee, and biscuit on the nightstand beside my bed and started propping up pillows. I had them all set except for one. I flipped one pillow over my head and down my back. But I misjudged the distance and hit my coffee with the edge of the pillow. It went everywhere.

As I screamed at myself and the world, I grabbed for the cup and hit the orange juice. It too went sprawling. Now I had both coffee and orange juice spilled on the table, on me, and on the bed. It took me forever to get it all cleaned up.

After that fiasco I was hungry again, so I fixed myself something to eat. I put the dishes and all that I used into the dishwasher. I had a hard time fitting it all in because the dishwasher was full. Later it dawned on me that all the things in the dishwasher might be clean and I had piled dirty dished on top of good.

I figured if they had been washed once it wouldn't hurt to wash them again, but I couldn't find any dishwasher detergent. So when you are out of one thing you improvise with another. The closest thing I could find to dishwasher detergent was the Palmolive we use in the sink with dishes. So I poured some of this into the spot where the detergent goes.

I turned on the machine and went upstairs for a nap. When I woke up I went downstairs and the entire kitchen floor was covered with bubbles. Fluff, the cat, had taken to higher ground and was perched on one of the kitchenette chairs. She appeared to be in shock. So was I.

It took me twice as long to clean up this mess as it did the coffee spill. But I had everything back shipshape before Terry got home from work. She didn't notice anything at first, but she later did say something about how clean the kitchen floor looked.

Aliens among Us

Sometimes I feel like I am a stranger on this planet. Do you know what I mean? Often after I have digested the newspaper or looked at the news on television I get the feeling I really don't belong here. I look at the focus of horrendous stories and think, "Who on earth are these people?"

It seems like every day there is something new to stagger the mind. Just when you think you have heard, read, or seen it all, something new pops up to make you know you haven't. Then you look at your relatively quiet life and you wonder how things have gotten so far out of hand.

Recently, I stayed at home from work because I wasn't feeling my best. I turned on the TV to pass the time. Believe me there is not much on TV to help you pass the time. However, I did see a show that caught my interest. It concerned teachers who are suing their students.

In several instances teachers had been harassed or threatened by students and had found no support from their school administration in handling the problem. So, fed up, they sued the children who were running amok in their classes. And in both of the cases highlighted on this show, the teachers were victorious.

Now, has it come to that? Have we let things get so far out of hand that we have to have teachers resorting to lawsuits in order to be protected! I'm amazed by this turn on events, and I feel like a stranger on earth.

When I was in school the teacher's word was law. Now there were some disciplinary problems to be sure but never anything of the level we are hearing about now. Even the frailest of teachers, and we had some who looked to be on their last legs, had the full support of the principal. All they had to do was say the word and we were out of there.

One of our teachers was a lady named Marjorie Hamilton. Rumor had it that at one time she had been a model in New York. We could never get confirmation of that fact. Anyway, her days as a model were past but she still acted and dressed the part. She spoke very softly, wore scarves around her neck at all times, and walked with each foot placed directly in front of the other.

She also used a nasal inhalant constantly. The poor lady had allergies. As she taught us French she would talk a while and then squeeze the inhaler, talk awhile and squeeze the inhaler, and on it would go until the hour was up.

Foolishly she left the inhaler on her desk in the afternoon. One day someone, who was never identified, snuck into the classroom, took that inhaler, and filled it with ink. The next day when the lecture started Miss Hamilton took her first sniff and sprayed her right nostril. She dabbed at it with a tissue never looking down at the evidence of ink running from her nose. It took two sprays before she caught on and then she nearly fainted. She ran from the room and soon Mr. Bannister, the principal, appeared.

The guilty party never confessed but the entire class had to write a paper on respect. And it was graded—severely—and became part of our semester average.

Now should we have treated Miss Hamilton that way? Of course not. But was it innocent fun compared with today's activities, of course!

The world keeps on changing and I feel like a stranger in it.

A Musical Miracle

Christmas and miracles have always been associated. It just goes with the season. So in anticipation of the upcoming Christmas season let me tell you of a miraculous occurrence.

It all started months ago when Stephanie Leonard asked if I would sing at her wedding. When Stephanie asked me, the wedding was a year or more away and I knew I would have plenty of time to practice. Plus, Stephanie is the type of young woman who's almost impossible to say no to at any time.

Her parents, Tom and Joanne, have been two of our best friends since we moved to Perry. We watched Stephanie and her sister Allison grow up just as they watched our two boys do the same. The Leonards moved to Augusta a couple of years ago and I'm still grieving. But we have remained close friends.

Anyway, Stephanie and her fiancé, Bill Yarborough, were getting married in Charleston, South Carolina, on Thanksgiving weekend. Stephanie had requested that I sing "The Lord's Prayer." Now "The Lord's Prayer" is not the easiest song in the world to sing, but I did get a tape of the music and rehearsed to and from work every day.

I got pretty good at hitting the high notes and sang it to my wife one day as we were traveling to Macon to a movie. My wife said it sounded pretty good, and I agreed. The problem, I told her was that it only sounded good in the car. Whenever I tried it outside the car it sounded lousy. She suggested I have the church people run a microphone out to my car at the wedding and sing it that way. Either that or lip-sync it, but I didn't think the people at St. Phillip's Episcopal Church in Charleston would go for that.

Finally, the time came for us to go to Charleston. I was still sounding good in the car. But when we got to the rehearsal and I met the organist I was bundle of nerves. He suggested we try it with organ accompaniment. We did. I cracked on notes and sounded like chalk on the blackboard. Children and animals for miles were screaming in pain.

Next, we moved to the piano. There it sounded a little better on the first go through. On the second it was back to cruelty to animals. He suggested that he try to lower it a key. I agreed gratefully. This time we did get through it.

By the time for the wedding the next day I was a wreck. Everybody in the wedding party had been so gracious to us. And Stephanie was so exited about my singing. I could just imagine her horror when I cracked on the opening notes.

Finally, it was time for the wedding to start. The procession of groomsmen and bridesmaids began.

I began to tear up when I saw Allison walking down the aisle as her sister's maid of honor. She was radiant. And then there was Stephanie coming down on Tom's arm. If ever there was picture-book bride, it was she.

Now I began to pray in earnest. I started with pleading, then bargaining, and then anything if God would just get me through the song. I told Him I just couldn't do it. I just couldn't get it out.

The reading of the scripture ended and it was my time to walk to the front of the altar and sing. I was shaking as I stood up but then a sense of peace filled me. When the piano started I was calmness itself.

As I opened my mouth to sing "Our Father" a voice came out of me that was not mine. It was controlled, calm, and on key. It flowed forth and filled the church. It was beautiful.

I know it is hard to believe but it really wasn't me singing that day. In my heart I know God sent a gift of love to Stephanie through me. And it was a miracle.

A New Year's Blessing

As the New Year of 1996 starts it is once again time to reflect on the status of the world, and on our own individual lives. Plus, it is time for prayers for peace, love, and harmony in our lives.

Have you really thought about the troops being sent to Bosnia? Aside from the arguments pro and con, have you really thought about the individuals who missed Christmas with their loved ones? Would you like for that to be you? I certainly wouldn't.

My holidays have been spent with worry about which gift to buy and what party to attend. There seemed to be a shortage of time to get everything done, but at least it was time spent surrounded by my friends and family. If I had been off in a foreign land and alone, it would have been horrific.

It also seems to me that at this time of the year and at this time in my life, I am more aware of the sadness that comes with hardships of the elderly. I look at my parents and marvel at their abilities to carry on day after day as one problem becomes ten, and ten become one hundred. Yet they still manage to be upbeat and cheerful when I speak to them by phone.

My father becomes more and more frail of body but the growth of his spirit is staggering. He still knows what life is about and holds on to each moment as much as he can. As for my stepmother, she has entered sainthood. Day after day, moment after moment, she is there taking care of my father. And doing it with patience, love, and total compassion. God bless her, God bless her, God bless her.

I also have reflected on the good things of the past years. I don't know of anywhere else I would rather live than Perry. I like knowing the people in the grocery store. I like having a church home where I am surrounded by my friends. I appreciate having a neighborhood that is quiet and safe and comfortable.

I am sure people living in Warner Robins, Fort Valley, Byron, Centerville, Bonaire, Elko, etc., feel the same way about their communities, but for me, Perry can't be beat. I was at a function a few weeks ago and somebody teasingly said I lived in MayPerry (as in Andy Griffith's Mayberry) and I took it as a compliment. Life here is more ordinary in the most special sense of the word.

There are also special people in my life who mean more and more to me. I love each and every one of the people I work with. We are a small group, but everybody pulls together and is concerned about each other. It is a special office with special workers.

I also especially love my Sunday school at the Methodist church. I have been in the same class for twenty-something years and have enjoyed every Sunday I have spent with this group of people. They are a community of believers who exemplify the most positive aspects of Christianity.

It would not be possible for me to reflect on the blessings of my life without mentioning my family. Why God chose to bless me with total happiness in my marriage and with my children, I do not know. There are other people who are much better than I who have bad marriages and troublesome kids. But I got the best, and at least I have the sense to know it.

So have yourself a wonderful 1996 full of the best life can offer. Savor it to the fullest, and share it with all your loved ones. Save something for the poor, the sick, and the unfortunate, too.

Epilogue

So here we are, still on the road, and the sun is still shining overhead. The memories gathered still cling to us like dust on our clothes. We are a little older, a little wiser, and a little weary. Still the excitement of tomorrow beckons.

Who knows what the rest of the "journey" will bring, but if the second half is anywhere close to the first, it is going to be a wonderful trip. I am still healthy, happy, and hopeful, and I have my eye on new goals and new horizons.

It is exciting to ease on down the road and find new friends, new experiences, and new adventures. I will try to keep the best friends and experiences of my life with me, and open myself up to finding new joys in the future. With family, friends, and faith the journey will be pure pleasure. I hope yours is too.

Until next time, keep the sun in your face, the wind at your back, and a lot of hope in your heart.